Prayer For My Son – by Elizabeth Gan

Copyright© 2012 Elizabeth Gan

Signpost books

Redding, CA

www.Signpostbooks.com

www.Prayerformyson.com

ISBN 978-0-9853642-0-5

Library of Congress Control Number: 2012905574

Cover background image by Suriyaphoto from Createstime.com

Cover graphics and design by Elizabeth Gan

Prayer for my Son

By Elizabeth Gan

<u>Dedications</u>

To Jordan: Son, I am so so so proud of who you are, and I love you so much. I am privileged beyond words to be your mother here on earth. You are the most wonderful thing to come into my life, and I am honored to know you. Simply said, I love you, son.

Acknowledgments

Bill and Beni Johnson: Words often fail me when I think of you two, while other times I could fill a whole book telling you how much you have done for us and how honored we are to know and love you. It is one of the greatest privileges of my life to call you friends. Daddy Bill, who you are every moment of every day is inspirational to me. I am floored by your humility and character. Where would we be without you?. Beni, my friendship with you is priceless and precious, and I wouldn't be where I am if you had not scooped me up. Thank you for being my friend and loving us both. You guys have changed my life forever, and I am eternally thankful for you two. I will always have the privilege of having your backs and I love you, I love you, I love you.

Bethel Church, Redding California: You are the best family and group of hungry people pursuing God that I could ever have hoped to know. You are heaven on earth to me. I am proud of being in this family.

To Darlene Zschech and the Hillsong worship team: When you guys sing, your hearts of love for God permeate your words, till there is no room for anything else but adoration. I have every album you guys have made and have proudly worn them all out! They have been my signpost pointing me to worship him, while walking through the hardest and darkest places and the good times, too. Thank you for all you have done, for all the countless hours of writing, leading, traveling and hard work. Thank you, thank you.

Pam Spinosi, your friendship and support have made this journey easier. Thank you for your love and help. I love you, Cuz!

Dear Papa God...

Hey it's me, your favorite child here!! As this whole book is about you and me, I thought that you should have your own page of dedication. So Tada. Here it is Papa.

Seriously, from the first moment we met all those years ago, I will never EVER forget the light of your face. You had me at that first glance! I am yours....

I'm told I sang before I spoke, and I worshiped and danced before I walked! I was yours from the moment I popped out into the world (poor world, didn't see me coming). I have known you for what feels like eternity and shall continue to. From the very first breath I took, to my last, I will never stop singing and loving on you. I will never be satisfied enough to not pursue you anymore, and my hunger will never wane for more of your presence. You have been the sole purpose behind every breath, every hug I gave, every song I have sung. And I truly, madly, deeply love you, God.

Oh, also, thanks for leaving Holy Spirit down here! Sheesh, it would be so boring without him, eh!! We like him a lot and he is so much fun! ☺

THANK YOU for the cross, Jesus. You say it was all worth it because being able to spend eternity with me is fun, so I thank you for not giving up, keeping strong till the end and for everything you have done.

Although this story was hard to write out, I did it for you and for hope.

I hope you like the book, Papa, and that people see you in every page.

Your brown-eyed girl,

Liz

Forward by Beni Johnson

Pain or suffering is never something that any of us wants in our lives. Many may think that there should never be those elements in our walk here on earth. But life happens, and we live on a planet that is not perfect and full of pain and suffering. Really, what counts in life when there is pain and suffering is how we choose to go through it. God never told us that we would never have to go through the pain of life, those things that are so unjust and are just wrong! But He did promise to never leave us or forsake us. To me that is a precious promise that we all need to hold onto when life takes a turn on us. Our Daddy God will never leave us alone! His presence to comfort us and keep us in the palm of his hand is a precious gift for us. I met Liz Gan at a prophetic school that my church Bethel in Redding, California, has every year. She came up to me and introduced herself to me and we talked. We met, but more than that, our spirits met. At that time I had no idea what was happening or had happened in her life. All I knew was that I really liked her. As our friendship grew, she became a very important part of my life. She has covered me and my husband in prayer and was, and still is, committed to us. Eventually some things happened in her life and she packed up her son and her life and moved to Redding to be in our church.

In this book Liz exposes her heartache and longing for her son Jordan's healing. Along the way she receives insight and revelation. It is like God is holding her hand through the long and continual process of seeing the healing come.

One of the valuable lessons in our lives is the lesson in learning the power of declaration. I highly respect Liz for many reasons, but one is that there was a shift in her spirit, and she learned this lesson of seeing who you are or who her son was to be and declaring that over him. No matter what was told to her by the doctors or people, she knew that there was an answer. So, she went to her heavenly Father, our great physician, and asked. God never fails us, and in her asking and surrendered heart, He came and gave her the tool of declaration. He showed her the way that he had created Jordon to be.

This story, *Prayer for my Son*, is full of promise and faith of a young mother who chose against all odds to believe in something that she knew but could not see yet. Jordan is still walking out his healing. It is an ongoing miracle but I have to tell you it is a miracle, period. It is the hand of a loving heavenly Father who has come down and is still coming to bring healing to a special young man of God.

Thank you, Liz, for this book. I am so proud of you. It is truly an honor to know you and call you my friend.
Love to you always,

Beni Johnson
Author of *The Happy Intercessor*

Introduction

My son and I experienced a miracle of healing. That's when I decided to write it out, because so many people wanted to read of our account. It seemed like a simple thing to do, to write it down. I mean how hard could it be? But it turned out to be one of the hardest things I have ever done. When I started writing, I realized that I was in the middle of my journey and not at the end like I had once thought. I thought that it was finished and that God was done working on us, but he wasn't. Along the journey things got very hard. There were set backs and trials, but one of the hardest parts that was towards the end of the healing manifesting, my marriage broke apart. I was left to parent my son alone.

The journey of writing it out down started when I, in a moment of passionate expression, uttered a promise to God. I said, "If you heal my son, I am going to go after this thing." I meant what I said whole-heartedly, but you never can predict just how or what God uses to work things out in your life.

That one prayer has been one of the hardest things I have prayed so far in my life. I had no way of knowing what that promise looked like fulfilled or the cost of it. In reality, it did cost me a lot: a lot of time, sleep, normal friendships, living a normal life, etc. I would like to say that it was simple—I prayed a few prayers, Jordan was healed and boom, our new life began! The book wrote itself and it was all good. But that isn't true. The journey of writing this book and watching his healing manifest were tied together. Along the way I experienced regresses in Jordan's healing as if it were a tug of war with the enemy.

No sooner had I written a breakthrough down than the ugly tug of war began and it was a battle of faith and stubborn persistence. There was not a day that went by that I didn't hear the devil call me a liar or have him try to push doubts into my mind about my promise and who God is and what he could do. The closer we got to the finish line, the harder it got to push on through. I didn't know if it was ever going to end or know when I could say, "It is finished."

Writing this all out and talking to people who also want the same breakthrough, has made my heart break again. It doesn't bring you any joy to look at someone who is struggling with the same thing as you, in so much pain and not just fix it for them in an instant. I don't want anyone to be living in lack or sickness, but I also don't want our testimony to end up just being a simple formula for people to use. A formula takes the need for relationship out of the situation, and one thing I know more than anything else is that God is all about relationship. The thing you can never by-pass in God's miracles is relationship. I can tell you what I did and how, why or when even, and that may help you, but that is not my main desire. My desire is that at the end of this book you will be motivated by love to seek after God, despite your circumstances.

While I cannot impart my history with Jesus to you and the roads we traveled to get where we are today, it is from our journey into the heart of God that we got our breakthrough. If I had not gotten hungry and made a decision to go after God first, then this would not have happened. My aim is not to provide you a formula and solution, but some hope, that nothing is too difficult for God. As you read through my journey with Jordan and God, I also pray that it gives you a hunger to know him more than you have before.

What I desire is that this story, these words and my life, will become a signpost. A signpost, after all, should not be a place to stop and park, with the hope that the words on the board are the destination. The words on a signpost are merely a description of the destination. They point in the direction to go. So I point you towards the Father's heart; it is there that you will find your answers.

Chapter 1

It begins with a question

"Would you still love me and stay with me if I never healed your son, Liz?"

I could not answer the Lord for a few moments.

When I heard those words, I was walking down the hallway into my living room, laundry basket in hand, toys waiting to be cleared away. Time stood still as I heard him say that to me. At first I didn't believe I heard correctly, so I put everything down and asked him, "What did you say, Lord?"
His voice came through clearer than if He was standing right next to me, and he repeated his question in his soft voice, "Would you stay with me if I never healed your son?"

Shock hit me and I didn't know how to respond. I dropped to my knees in a puddle of tears after hearing his almost audible voice that reverberated through not only my being but the whole house. I had no doubt that God was speaking to me. What I heard in his voice was not a demand, not a king's decree or a question. It sounded like a friend who was reaching out for my heart. The sound in his voice, the question from his heart, made me examine my own heart and contemplate a question that would change my life.

I stopped and surveyed my situation. I examined my heart and thought about what our future would look like, and I honestly didn't know if I could actually carry on with the way things were. I didn't want to live in this survival mode for the rest of my life, but I had come to a crossroad.

The choice was between the road of merely surviving life, parenthood and whatever this was that had gripped my family, or the road to deeper intimacy in God and the possibility of it not improving at all for us. Which path should I choose? What was I going to say back to him?

I was speechless and was struggling to find something to say to the Lord in the midst of a rush of emotions. I felt him expectantly waiting for me to answer. Why did he ask me that question? All I wanted was for him to wave his mighty hand and give me the instant "fix it" solution to my problem. That was, after all, God's job, wasn't it? From my point of view, I had been praying for the solution for a while now and had done all that I knew I could on my side, so now it was really up to God, and yet he asked me to choose. I was confused!

I could not ignore the openness in his voice; it made him sound so real and vulnerable. The tone in his words were not authoritative, ordering me to do something or else, but sounded like it was from a genuine friend to friend position. I wanted things desperately to be different than they were and yet, here I was, blindsided by a question from heaven that started to expose the inner thoughts and feelings I had towards God. How could it be that one little question could shake me to the core of my theology and expose expectations of Him?

I went and sat down on the couch, sorting through the mess of emotions and scenarios running like a racecar through my head. Why couldn't I answer Him right away? Why had He answered my question with another question, leaving the ball in my court? After calming down a little, the first reaction I had going through my head was one that made me sound like I was a two-year-old stomping her feet and having a tantrum! It stank of self-pity and emotional and physical exhaustion. The second reaction closely resembled the first and also reeked of anger at not getting my way. I didn't want to give God an answer based on a childish soul reaction and then later change my mind. Reactions number three and four weren't much better, either!

So I stopped. I took a breath and just focused on why He would ask me that in the first place. How could that one question make me react in that way? Why could I not just give Him the right answer I knew He wanted and was theologically best? Maybe God didn't want theology? Maybe He wanted my heart instead?

I replied, "Lord, I don't like that question. It hurts, but I need some time to think about it."

He graciously answered, "Okay."

As I heard my son begin to stir from his nap, I felt God smiling at me as though he agreed to wait for my answer. I carried on with laundry, childcare, cooking and cleaning, but all throughout, I had that hard question running through the back of my mind. I had known the Lord long enough to know what my answer could or should be, but I was at that crossroad where my desperation overtook my theology, and they were locked in a wrestling match.

Was it to be the possibility of life without the healing I desperately prayed to manifest for my son, and in exchange, more of God than I had experienced before? Or was it going to be that the need for a healing surpassed my love for God and I would be in a relationship with God that would never go deeper if I didn't let go?

The answer is simple really to the average person who has a history with God, simple to the person who has not been faced with a crushing desperation for healing. I had never had a problem with that kind of a question before. Previously, whenever God asked me for something that was uncomfortable, challenging or stretching, I never denied him and readily agreed to whatever he wanted. Yet, somehow this time, it was different. I had to go away to think about it, process it through my mind and imagine what life was going to be like if things stayed the same. I also imagined that if I made the wrong, selfish choice, it was going to hurt God and I could not stand that.

In the end, I thought about it for what felt like an eternity. In reality, only a few hours had passed before I came to a satisfactory conclusion. I knelt down on the carpet on my living room floor and asked for Holy Spirit to come. His presence just flooded my being and my house and amidst the tears pouring down my face, I offered him my answer.

I said to the Lord, "Absolutely, I would stay with you, no matter what."

I felt a release and a joy. I smiled from ear to ear because I knew that God had the answer that he wanted and it came with all my heart and honesty. That was it, simple as that. I didn't ask what the next years would look like for us if things didn't change. I didn't picture what next week was going to be like or how I should plan ahead. I wasn't sure how I would survive whatever this thing that had hit our family, but I released my expectations of him, focused on his face and got on with my day.

When I thought about it later on in the day, I realized that I was not happy with where my relationship with God was and that it wasn't working as well as it should. I knew I was saved, filled with the Holy Spirit, had been water baptized and had read my Bible from cover to cover. I prayed in tongues and had many encounters with God as a child and throughout my life. I had always wanted to be a missionary or in full-time ministry, but somehow this was not the mission field that I had expected or trained for. Somehow this mission field was the hardest assignment I think he could ever have given me. Rumbling through islands and jungles for Jesus seemed easier than what lay before me.

This rocked my core, and with it, my relationship with God. I could not reconcile this hole in my faith. It had somehow gotten to being about works instead of a relationship with him. That question moved me back into place with no guarantee of anything other then his love.
But from the moment that I had given my answer to him, I felt different inside my heart, and I knew I had crossed a turning point in my life with God. I wasn't in a relationship with him to get something from him; I was in it for him. If he never did anything for me again, that was okay.

If I never heard his voice again or saw another miracle, that was fine. Just being with him, without the trimmings was pure heaven, and I had somehow forgotten that along the way. The decision I had just made me feel free inside, and a new peace saturated my mind. It was now not my problem to try to nag God into healing my son. The strings that I had attached through expectations were severed. I no longer saw God through my childish eyes as the Daddy that gave me everything I wanted, when I wanted it.

For the next few days, things were normal for us, same routine and same troubles to deal with. We went on living in survival mode and dealt with each minute as it came. I could not imagine what ten minutes into the future looked like, let alone how we were going to get through a week. That was just the way we had gotten used to living.

Suddenly something started to change, and not in the way that I thought it would. There were no flashes of light with the heavens opening and angels appearing, singing with harps. My son didn't sit up, look at me, and say, "Hello Mommy, how are you today?" The struggles that we fought with every day simply stayed the same. Although I always looked for changes in Jordan, they honestly didn't come then. The change began in me, first. Before, I had just wanted my situation to change so I could get closer to God again and get back to the normal life I had before. I wanted God to come and sort this all out for me so I could waltz back into Easyville with no effort on my part.

But God, instead of changing a situation for me, had another approach, one that I didn't want to hear about because it didn't fit in my plan. He went straight for me, instead of my situation. I began to see that God was into empowering people to change things, rather than doing it all for them. He didn't force himself on me and invade my will and move me like a puppet on a string without my consent. If he wanted puppets, he would have made puppets. If he wanted robots, he would have made robots, but he made humans instead with free wills. He made children in his own image. That means we have a choice; we have options to choose from.

God came in close. Instead of him giving me a hand out or a quick fix to help me out, he wanted to give me a hand up and empower me through relationship with him, so I could move my own junk out of the way.

It was the beginning of the journey into the Father heart of God.

A year earlier, my son was diagnosed with Autism/Asperger's Syndrome, severe allergies and severe hyperactivity when he was nearly 2 years old.

Chapter 2

Back to the beginning

I had a relatively normal pregnancy. There were a couple of times where some minor things happened, but in the end it was fairly normal. He decided to be different and be in a breech position so I had a scheduled cesarean section. From the moment he was born, he looked like he was absolutely ready to take on the world. He stared calmly around the room and had this incredible countenance of peace about him. He lay on the table as he was weighed and measured, poked and prodded, but he just stared at me as if he was waiting for me to hold him. Then they handed him to me and I was extremely happy. I knew my life would never be the same again.

Life in the first few weeks was a little crazy, with my healing from the C-section and forming schedules. Jordan had no problems eating and sleeping and all the other things newborns do. I could not believe just how amazing he was and how in love with him I was. Pregnancy and motherhood are absolute miracles! There he was, this little baby forming inside me, and suddenly, poof, out he pops with a whole soul and spirit and life ahead of him. Like any new parent, I took a while to get used to things.

I didn't have family around to help or to give me advice, so for the most part, I was on my own navigating each day as it came. Weeks turned into months and we settled into having a newborn in the house, and like most new parents, our house resembled a cross between a huge laundry pile and a Toys-R-Us store.

As Jordan started to grow, things initially seemed to go well. A few months later, he started to get really fussy for no apparent reason.

I knew that he was growing and changing, getting used to life on the outside. But I had a gut feeling that this was a little different. I could not comfort him or seem to calm him down. I knew babies cry and especially with teething or colic, but still it was a bit scary to hear him scream so much as a new mother. In a matter of months he went from being a calm child to one who was red-faced and unable to breathe from screaming so hard. When it got to that point, I could not calm him down no matter what I tried and it went on for hours. I tried everything I knew but nothing seemed to work. At that early stage, I asked the doctor for help or directions, but everything they suggested we had tried and didn't seem to work. I didn't know what to do or how long this phase would last.

At first, it started off as just a few moments of screaming fits when he was hungry or tired, pretty normal really. But then, it developed into an hour or two of crying, which then turned into three hours straight red faced screaming for no apparent reason (even though I had done everything I could). Fussy didn't quite seem to describe him and he began crying into the night as well. Before, he was going down easily and sleeping well; now he could not sleep at night at all. His naps disappeared completely and suddenly during the days, so now he was not only tired from no naps, but unable to sleep at night either. And no matter how much I held him, or what I tried to do to calm him down, nothing worked.

Over a period of time, the child that I once knew only a few months earlier just seemed to slip slowly away. He went from being a very sweet, happy baby to being a very fussy, difficult one. The mother's "maybe" questions hit me. Maybe it was that his little personality was changing and growing or that he was going through a growth spurt?

Maybe he was just teething? Maybe I ate something that he didn't like and it was coming through the breast milk? Maybe he had a cold or didn't like the weather changes? I knew that there would be times when he would be fussy and I just took it as a short-term thing and tried to make him comfortable and happy. But somewhere deep inside of me, I had a feeling that something else was wrong. This wasn't just growth spurts or teething or even colic, there was something beneath his eyes.

Most people would say that was normal. I thought so, too at first, and at the time I rolled with the punches and tried to be flexible. But as the months went by and he got worse, I wasn't so sure anymore. He spent sometimes up to twelve hours a day screaming and crying, and I could do nothing to stop him or make him happy, anymore. Honestly, I thought I was the worst mother in the world and that it was all my fault. As this was my first child I was still learning how to care for an infant. Maybe I wasn't doing enough or maybe I was doing lots of things wrong.

I tried different diets, walks, driving and music, and nothing seemed to ease anything at all. Advice from everyone I knew poured in. Doctors gave me the usual help all of which I had already done. My mother told me what she did; I asked friends and tried to come up with a plan to help or an explanation as to what was making him so upset all the time. He just would not stop crying or fussing all day.

Within a few months after he was born, he suddenly and mysteriously became allergic to my breast milk. He would start off feeding well but then would have an immediate upset stomach while he was eating, and for hours afterwards he would scream. By the time I had cleared things up from the last feeding and he had finally calmed down, it was time for another feeding. I just didn't know what I was doing wrong. I tried different positions while feeding him. I changed my diet and made everything quiet while he ate. When the quiet didn't seem to help, I played music while he fed. I tried different bottles and different nipples for those bottles. I tried every formula on the market but with no improvement. We even bought goats' milk, rice milk, and soymilk, but the screaming, fussiness, hives around his mouth and belly, and diarrhea continued, no matter what we gave him to eat.

I spent most of my time researching and testing what he was seemingly reacting to or what made him happy. I drove him around town, swung him in his car seat for hours, walked around my apartment like it was a running track. I rocked him. I sang to him. I did everything I could to try to calm this little one down. I waited and changed everything I could; I avoided things that I thought would make it worse, but to no avail.

The night times proved to be the most challenging and grew to be more tiring than the days. He ended up not sleeping unless one of us held him all night and rocked him in a certain position and walked him in a particular pattern around his bedroom floor. If we did not, he would work himself up, and in the end, we would all be up the entire night. Even when he had spent a large portion of the night crying instead of sleeping, he still would not easily take naps during the day, although it was much needed for all of us.

I noticed that he was extremely hyperactive even as a young baby, and I would usually have to hold his legs and arms still for him during nap time for him to actually fall asleep and stay holding them for up to 30 minutes afterwards. It was like his legs did not have the ability to stop moving and his muscles were rock solid. His calf muscles were cramped constantly and his tendons were always tight. There was a time, when after days of no naps and hardly any sleep at night, that I noticed, too, that he could not even manage to shut his own eyelids. I had never seen that before, he would try to shut them and I would try to teach him peekaboo to help, but he could not close them willingly for naps. One time after days of no sleep I remember putting him down for a nap and helping his eyelids to shut so he could sleep! It was crazy to me that I had to do that because his body could not find a way to rest by itself. When I did hold his eyelids shut, he fell asleep in less than ten seconds and was snoring away!

One day in the middle of all this confusion, I noticed that Jordan's skin had little bumps on it after I fed him certain things. With how fussy he was and how much work it was to get him to eat, chew, and swallow without a tantrum and choking, I didn't notice this strange skin problem popping up silently, too. The bumps appeared all around his mouth or on his belly immediately as he ate his food or drank milk. Things that he had eaten the week before now made him have reactions. Then within minutes of eating, he began screaming and had diarrhea everywhere. I had never seen that before, so I took him to the doctor, who said it was just eczema. But I started to pay closer attention to what was going on with him as he ate. In addition to the hyperactivity and the need for constant movement, he began to itch and scratch away most of the day and night.

He scratched at himself till he bled because of those reactions. I saw the symptoms play off of each other like a pair of foes causing trouble; one would make worse the other symptoms. There were nights of sleeplessness, with scratching, kicking, screaming and bleeding. His hyperactivity made him move all the time, but the itching on his skin made him move also, so between the two he could not stop itching or moving.

One day I noticed that his already heightened sensitivity to average everyday things had gotten worse. I took him on one of our regular walks around our neighborhood in his stroller. The wind was blowing and the sun was shining and we were enjoying being outside. When we arrived back at the apartment, he was covered in hives and was screaming and scratching at himself. I could not imagine where he had gotten that kind of a reaction from. We didn't touch anything that he was normally allergic to, so I had no clue what had made him have that kind of a reaction. It was really puzzling to me as the week before we had done the exact same thing and nothing had happened. Why now? Our walks were once fun and it was nice to be out of the house, but now they were stressful and it was challenging to leave the house at all. Whether we were walking to the car, or going to the store, now I had to have that in mind whenever we walked anywhere, he could start to have a tantrum from scratching etc.

The next thing I noticed was that during his walk or an outing to a store, if I touched anything, such as a skin cream or a leaf, for example, and then touched him afterwards, it would cause red marks to come up on his skin. Slowly our world was becoming no bigger than the four walls of our house and it was beginning to feel like it was a prison. He was so sensitive that even if I would go out to buy laundry detergent or take him on a walk through a mall, the mere smells in the air suddenly made hives pop up on his face and body.

Subsequently, eczema started to cover his whole body. Grey skin covered the joints. Open bloody sores and old scabs dotted his body while rough red bumps filled the rest of his tiny frame. Once he had beautiful dark smooth baby skin, and then the next month it looked like grey scales, mixed with the constant bleeding from scars and scabs that never really had time to heal before another outbreak hit. His poor skin just never had a break from the itching and bleeding. Because of that, I couldn't use any kind of soap, shampoo, or cleanser on or even around him.

When it was bath time, I had to wash out the tub twice before he could use it because our shampoo residue or soap residue aggravated his bleeding skin. If one of us touched him and had any kind of skin cream or perfume on, or had touched something such as fruit even, and it would cause him to break out immediately and start to itch all over.

Jordan was too young to put steroid creams on, so we were unable to help him with medicated creams. Helplessly, we watched as he itched all day and cried as he scratched in minimal relief. All I could do was to wash or bath him several times a day and keep him as clean as possible. It meant careful washing of clothes in a special soap, and constant supervision.

I was on a constant look out for what he could and couldn't handle in his world. Foods that one day he could eat were suddenly the next day out of bounds: apples, oranges, pears, green beans, milk, cheese, eggs, anything. Foods that once he would have had fun chomping down on, now would bring him out in hives and itching in his mouth or lips and underneath his skin. The worst reaction he had was from peanut butter. I saw his face immediately blow up and hives cover his body; he was screaming and trying to breathe, and it was really scary. After that, no nuts of any kind were allowed anywhere near him or in the house. He was so sensitive to nuts that if he went into a house, restaurant or a store isle that had them, he would start to have an immediate reaction and we would have to leave.

When he did have a reaction to something, it would raise his heart rate, which, in turn, affected his already over tired and hyperactive body. It caused him to be sometimes incoherent and distracted by the discomfort, so much so that he was unable to hear us or talk to us.

As the number of his allergies grew, I started to compile a list, but there was no way to avoid everything on that list. No matter what I did or didn't do, no matter where I went or if I completely stayed at home for days, something always ended up happening, and he would have some sort of a reaction every day.

So our list of problems pilled up one by one, and as I struggled to find solutions for each one, the balance of his life seemed to never be plumb right. Milk allergy, food allergy, environmental allergy, hyperactivity, colic, teething, no naps, not sleeping at night, screaming fits during the day, eczema and constant hives. What was going on? Life with a new baby shouldn't be that hard, should it? What was I doing wrong? What have I done wrong? All I knew was that one day he was fine and the next, he was screaming in pain and I could do nothing for him.

I started to observe and protect him like a hawk. Everything that came into contact with him, and I mean everything, I looked at and even tested. I looked at food, air filters, music, tree pollen, grass pollen, chemicals in cleaning products, smells and creams, soap, bath waters, food and drink. I turned into one of those people who stand there for hours reading the backs of packages to see what was in them before they buy them, and I don't like shopping! The cupboards and all their contents in our house were reviewed in great detail. Every box and cleaning product was tested. I analyzed creams, foods, pollen in the air, trees, smells, cleaners, laundry detergent, soaps, and waters sources. The list of items Jordan reacted to was long and overwhelming.

Over that period of the first year or so, I tried everything I could think of. I changed his formula, tried different foods, moved to a new house, changed his laundry detergent, hand washed his clothes, and tried different eczema medicine. I tried music, rocking, walking and singing to him. I tried different cleaning products, air filters and special water for his formula and diet and baths and clothes. I even changed his bedding and painted his bedroom a different color, but nothing made any kind of difference. Music, quiet, loud, fans, massages, rocking, no rocking, praying in tongues, nothing worked. Still he was fussy and spent most of the day crying.

That was how we spent the first year and as the months went by, I had realized that somewhere in there, I had lost myself and my walk with God. I was only in survival mode and had gotten so busy trying to handle the baby and all the things thrown at us.

I was so preoccupied with cleaning up after throw ups and diarrhea, then trying to calm him, with hardly any sleep or breaks, and no other life. Spending time with God had taken a back seat, which made me even more frustrated. I knew having children was going to be hard work and that it would take a level of sacrifice that you can't really prepare for, but I felt so hopeless and useless.

I thought to myself, *I wonder if I can fix it? If I worked harder then would I be able to find out what was going on in him? What if I try to control everything he comes into contact with?* I started to blame myself for everything that was happening to him. Was I to blame? I asked myself what I had done and how I could fix this little person's life? Maybe if I tried harder and rocked him longer, fed him when he wanted, did everything he wanted me to do, stayed up all night rocking him the way he wanted, let him watch television all day, then maybe it would help to him calm down and everything would be all right.

We went to the doctor, and she said they could not find anything wrong with him other than obvious allergies, which we had him tested for. The blood test that we did do showed that he had no allergies whatsoever, but my observation was to the contrary. The doctor made suggestions of things we could try, all of which I had already done. And it seemed that I knew more than she did at that point, so I walked out of the office bewildered and feeling very alone. They just said he was a colicky baby and that he would probably grow out of it. I thought "Oh, okay. When? Please God, let it be soon!"

As Jordan turned a year old, I didn't see him interacting with us a lot. He only looked for us or for our attention when he needed something and would avoid me when I sat down to play with him. He would often scream for hours even as I held him, trying to comfort him or calm him down. He sometimes did not realize I was holding him at all, and he would stare off into the distance, crying. Normal physical touch either made him scream more or would go completely unnoticed. It was either too much for him to handle or was as if he wasn't feeling it at all.

I never knew which one was going to work, so all day I picked him up, massaged him, then put him down when he didn't want to be touched. He would scream at the tags on his clothes or the mere smell of the prints of t- shirts or pants. He would scratch away at the designs on clothing until I changed them.

Combined with his other skin allergies and upset stomachs, he was just not happy. With each mood change that lasted a few hours, I neither succeeded in calming him down or making anything better for him. But I had to try.

The other thing that was strange was that when I got toys out for him and tried to play with him, he would either start to scream at me and throw the toys at me or push them away or ignore them. The toys were not interesting to him, no matter how much I tried to engage him. Being creative didn't come naturally to Jordan. When I got the crayons out or something that required him to sit and activate his imagination, I had suddenly turned into the enemy of Jordan's universe. If he had imagination inside him, it was indeed locked within the confines of his brain. He only spent his energy and imagination on what he deemed important. Therefore, human interaction, playing with toys or conversation were not important or needed.

Sadly, I realized one day that the only time he was happy was when he had an electronic toy in his hand that made some kind of noise repeatedly or when the TV was on. I knew that it was unhealthy if that was all he was playing with, but there seemed to be a deep unhappiness in him that I could not fix. He was never really happy to see me. He didn't call out to me but instead ran to the TV, crying for it to be on. It would not have bothered me as much if he had social skills and wanted to play with me or other people or with other toys as well, but he didn't. He neither looked for human conversation, nor wanted it. He didn't want toys; he only wanted electronics. Human interaction had been replaced by electronics to the point that he didn't notice walls or when he walked into them, the people around him, or speech directed at him. He would not notice sounds that came from another source that wasn't electronic. He seemed oblivious to people or animals, if he was cold or hot, or if he was hungry or in pain. The world passed by without him noticing. I felt like I was banging on the door trying to get him to come out.

I remember the very first time he saw a TV program. He was around five months old and had been upset and was crying all morning. Finally, I decided that even though I hadn't eaten breakfast, showered or gotten properly dressed, we were going out for a drive and a change of scenery! I could not handle the confines of the four walls anymore.

I packed us up and got ready to go out for a drive. I strapped him in his portable car seat and left him in front of the TV. I turned it on to the Nickelodeon network while I walked upstairs to pack some things into the diaper bag. I suddenly heard a sound emanating from his mouth that I had not heard in a very long time. He was laughing, and I mean the deepest belly, giggling laugh I have ever heard. I ran downstairs to see what was happening. The children's show *Blue's Clues* was on and Jordan was giggling at Blue, the dog, prancing around the TV screen trying to find a clue. I turned it off as a little experiment and sure enough, the screaming fit started up as he stared at me as if to ask, "Why Mommy, why did you turn it off?" I turned it back on, and instantly he was happy again! I had not turned on the TV before this for him and was in awe at how easy it was to calm him down. It had the potential to quickly become an obsession as things often did with him.

I was reluctant to put the TV on during the day just to make him happy. When it was off, I noticed that he had started to hide himself away more in his little imaginary world and interacted less and less with me on the outside. I thought that it was his way of playing, by being creative or coping with the colic and allergies. I thought by my trying harder to engage him more, and by controlling his allergies with medicine, he would change, and I would have my happy baby back. But it didn't turn out that way.

Chapter 3

Extra jobs

When Jordan was about a year and a half old, we went to a clothing store in the evening and walked past a sign that had a picture of an owl on it. I was holding my son in my arms when he said loudly, "O-W-L. Owl." With all the noise in the store, I initially didn't notice that he was speaking. A few seconds later, I stopped in my tracks and asked, "What did you say, Jordan?" He screamed loudly at me because I was looking at him in the eye and talking to him. I asked him again what he said. He continued to fuss, so I kept moving and walked past another sign. Again, he said, "Owwlll." Pointing to a sign above a rack of clothing. I was astonished! He was spelling and speaking! At this point he had not spoken much to us and was mainly babbling as an 18 month old would do. How could it be that he could not even use words to tell me when he was hungry, tired, or in pain, yet he could spell a word? I was so confused that a child unable or willing to talk to me could, in fact, spell when I had not taught him letters properly.

At around four months old, he had started waking up at 4 a.m., cooing to himself in the crib as if it was wakey wakey time! I, on the other hand, did not feel that 4 a.m. was morning and would try to get him back to sleep, to no avail. He would spend most of the morning talking to himself, cooing day and night, and we thought it was the cutest sound ever. But from there it developed into a strange arrangement of incoherent pronunciations. He stayed at that incoherent and not understandable level, making no further progress. The doctors didn't seem concerned, so I thought he would talk when he was ready. But when he started to ignore us and get upset when I talked to him or looked him in the eyes, I felt like something else was going on in there. The day when he started to spell and speak, it showed that he was in fact very capable of listening and learning, but had trouble communicating.

The day after the "owl" situation, Jordan was cranky again and was refusing to nap as usual, so I tried to feed him a snack to calm him down. While he was sitting in his high chair, screaming bloody murder, I scribbled a number on a toy and turned it around to show him. He immediately stopped screaming and stared at the toy. I pointed to the number one and said, "One." I showed him my mouth as I wrote it out and repeated it a few times. Still stunned by the silence that was coming from the highchair, I carried on and said, "Two" and drew out the number. Then I grasped his face and got in close so he could only see my lip movement and said, "Two," again. Slowly and quietly out of his mouth, he said, "Oooneee." I stared at him in shock. He looked at me and then looked at the Magna-Doodle and looked away. A few moments later he said, "Ttttwooo." I was shocked and was so in awe of what was unfolding in front of me. He had not previously tried to mimic us, our speech or our actions in any way. He never copied our speech or looked at me when I talked to him, and for most of the day, my talking or interaction with him seemed to go unnoticed. By the end of the day he had learnt his numbers to 5 and a few letters. I had found a way to keep him happy and quiet, still and relaxed and I was going to use it!

As the days passed, I taught him numbers up to ten, the alphabet and then progressed to basic three-letter words. He grasped all those concepts in the matter of a few weeks. He was quickly spelling objects like "car" and "bus" that we saw as we were out and about. But I was still puzzled at how he could say "owl" and spell out the word as he had done in the store weeks earlier. I had no idea how he had learnt that or could speak that! But for sure there was something different about how he learned.

I could see that he had gaps in the foundations of his cognitive development. He could spell basic words, yet not read a book or enjoy being read to. He could not play with a toy and engage his imagination, work out how to feed himself, know the difference between when he was hot or cold, yet he could do things that were years ahead academically. I wondered why if he was capable of learning, labeling and interacting, that he could not rest, eat or walk properly? Why was he so angry at the thought of playing with toys with me or of me singing and playing music?

The distance between the two sides of his abilities was separated by a huge gap, and I didn't know what caused it or how to bridge it. I was puzzled by how he couldn't communicate hunger to us, or feel anything when he walked into a wall, but knew how to label the wall and spell it!

His speech developed differently. At first, he was speaking minimally but most of his speech came from repeating the lines of TV shows or from the electronic toys. He copied the sounds and lines as best he could but his pronunciation always sounded a little off, as if spoken through gritted teeth or a twisted tongue. When I asked him a question, he did not know what to say back to me, so he would babble at me or say something that was not understandable. Most often his response came in the form of a line from the TV show *Dora* or *Blue's Clues* that had no application to the question I had asked him. I would say "Jordan are you hungry?" and he would reply with a line from a show such as "a clue, a clue!" (from *Blues Clues*). I felt like he locked himself away from me and did not want to talk to me or listen. My heart was hurting, and I didn't know what to do.

His behavior after a while gradually became more strange, ever so silently that it's as if it crept up on us without our realizing and we had not realized just how different he was. Whereas he once looked in my eyes as a baby when I talked to him, now he stared at the wall, talking to himself, ignoring me. He avoided eye contact with me and with others. It was as if eye contact burned his eyes, and he could no longer tolerate it from anyone. At times, he would stare right through anyone who was talking to him, as if completely unaware that they were there. Other times, he would quickly look at a person, but their eyes would seem to scare him so much that he would pull back and look away while putting his hands over his eyes to shield himself and scream.

When he did finally want to talk to us, he would recite a TV episode from beginning to end with babbled speech and flapping of arms. He would repeat it word for word, line for line, after only watching it once. Even then, he would not look at me, only at the walls. This was the only response that I would often get from him when I tried to engage him in conversation. It seemed like he did not want to talk to me or couldn't let go of his imaginary world long enough to tell me when he was hungry or needed anything.

Conversations with him just could often not be understood, or he could not listen long enough to understand what I was saying.

At one point, I thought that maybe his hearing was damaged, so I had it tested often. The strange thing was that he heard everything from the cars pulling up in a driveway down the road to the toilets flushing next door! His hearing was so good that he could hear high frequencies outside of the average human range. Those sounds that would go undetected by others, would aggravate him and overwhelm his sensory system, sending him into screaming fits on the floor. At the sound of my worship CD's, he would flap his hands up and down and scream louder than the music, just to counteract it. He had the ability to hear any piece of electronic equipment go on anywhere in the house and would run to see what it was. It could have been my sewing machine, the washer, the TV or a laptop being switched on, but in any case, he would know what it was and immediately go find it. It then had his full attention, and he would not be able to walk away from it. I knew his hearing was good and very sensitive, but there was nothing I could do about the extra sensitivity other than put ear plugs in his ears all the time. His overloaded hearing made it difficult to get him to listen to me when I talked to him. Because of this he often chose electronics over human social interaction. So normal conversation passed him by.

Other everyday sounds like the microwave or vacuum cleaner aggravated him, making him dizzy, and would send him into fear-filled tantrums. I struggled to carry on with normal life inside the home. As much as possible, I tried tiptoeing and shushing everything in sight making it more livable for him, but it wasn't always successful. It seemed as if he was one great sound-processing conductor with no off switch. You could tell that the sounds he could not assimilate or process would aggravate his nerves and his muscles, leaving me helpless to do anything about it.

The world seemed to antagonize him constantly. He just didn't seem to fit. With all the sounds, the barrage of allergies, the constant itching and sneezing, upset stomachs and clean-ups, fussy food menus, no music or noises, limited playtime fun, and no naps, I simply could not keep up.

I could not figure out his mood from one moment till the next. At any moment, he would want the opposite of what he wanted just ten minutes before. I was constantly on my toes trying to make this little human happy. Most of the time he would want to be alone, sitting in the corner talking to himself and ignoring me or watching T.V. Other times, he would need me to hold him tightly, rock him, and massage his feet or hands in exactly the way he wanted for hours on end.

My new normal was that I never knew how Jordan was going to wake up feeling or who he was going to be, what he was going to act like and what he would remember from the day before. I knew that I would have no guarantee of what would work each day, what he would like to eat, what he wanted to do, or if he would take a nap or if he would scream for T.V all day long.

I started to notice other little strange physical signs that Jordan exhibited. He started to walk on his tiptoes, he would jump on the spot at anything that excited him or scared him, and he talked to himself for hours on end while staring at the wall, sometimes rocking himself. He also endlessly flapped his hands in response to happiness or frustration. He could not communicate with words, but just jumped up and down screaming or babbling while flapping his hands. Often, he would hit his hands on furniture or other things because he would not be paying attention to where he was while flapping his hands up and down. For hours on end, he would sit rocking, or stand still staring at things, or jump on his tiptoes and flap his arms till they were cold or had no feeling in them. He looked like a bird trying to fly with excitement, but it was so hard to watch.

At first all these things popped up so subtly that I didn't notice them gradually become the overwhelming majority to his normal style of his life. Other people who watched thought all his little ways were cute and funny, pointing at him, staring and giggling. But it hurt me deeply. I would just smile or walk away because they had no idea at all. To me it wasn't cute, after years of being ignored by my own child, having people point and stare, laugh even at him/us, it was way past funny.

When he started to flap his arms more and more, it eventually caused him to lose feeling in his hands. When he wasn't flapping them, he could not open his hands; they grew cold and clammy and were constantly in the shape of a ball. He would make a fist and be unable to open his hands by himself. I had to pry them open every few minutes during the day and massage the open hand to get his feeling back into his fingertips. Something was going on that I needed help with; parts of his body were completely numb while others were super sensitive. His head was so sensitive to touch, yet his limbs were almost completely without feeling yet muscles were so tight from cramping. I could not touch his torso without him squirming and laughing or screaming.

Things like walking had started to become hard for him. Initially, he developed normally; walking just after a year or so and went from crawling to running in no time. He walked straight and strong, was balanced and had good feet formation. He had met all of the doctors' goals in growth charts, but then one day, when he was about 2+ years old, he stopped walking properly. He stopped talking to me, he stopped looking at me in the eye. When he walked he either fell over his feet or only ran sideways. Somehow, he could no longer put one foot in front of the other, or keep his balance walking while looking at the world around him.

He could run while flapping his arms and looking at the floor, but he could not walk with his hands down by his side calmly down a path. He ended up running everywhere all the time whether it was into a busy street or in a store. He was unable to walk at a normal pace and would get really annoyed at me for making him slow down. However, when he ran, he neither looked up nor listened to what was around him. Many times, he would take off running in a parking lot or store aisle and run straight in the path of an oncoming car or shopping cart.

When we went out, I had to remind him constantly to look where he was going, I had to help him practice walking every day. I went through a period when wherever we went, I knelt in front of him and physically directed his feet. I helped him place his feet one in front of the other while I held his head in place and tried to get him to look where he was going.

People stopped and stared, pointed and laughed at me, but I knew he needed training to walk along a street without falling or constantly walking out in front of cars or into things. He could not handle the distractions from the noisy traffic or people walking and talking around him.

Because he walked constantly on his tiptoes, I found his tendons in his ankle and calf muscles were rock hard and cramped all the time. I had to massage his calf muscles to try to release some of the tension in them. But the massages would hurt him because of the cracked, bleeding skin from the eczema that covered his legs. I worked with his ankles and tendons every day, stretching them out and massaging them as often as I could get him to stop jumping.

It was always a lot of work leaving the house and going somewhere. On one outing, Jordan noticed an automatic sliding door at a store for the first time. I had just planned on popping out for a few food items but it turned into another one of those trips where he would get stuck on something and it birthed a new obsession. When we left the car and I helped him walk as usual positioning his head straight out in front of us and placed his feet ready to walk, he heard a sound that was interesting to him. The automatic sliding door. He was fascinated to be able to open the door by jumping on the mat in front of the door. It was funny in the beginning to see him get so much joy out of playing with a door. It brought a smile to many people's faces to see a child enjoy a door too, but after the fourth or fifth time, it wasn't so cute anymore. By the fortieth time Jordan jumped on the mat to open the door, and nearly 30 minutes later, it was way past funny. It often meant that he would stay outside the store and would not go in without a screaming fit. Once we were inside, he would only stare back at the door wanting to go back or finding a way to get back to it. He would scream if I put him in the cart, or he would walk straight into other people, displays, and carts because his attention was always on the sliding door. If I picked him up and carried him then I couldn't carry the items I needed to get from the shelves, so there was my dilemma!

Another annoying habit he developed next after going to the store was that we would come back home with a whole slew of conversations and sounds that he had heard while being out.

He would then get home and repeat them for hours on end, things that I couldn't understand. Everything he heard came back with him and repeated through his head like on a circuit—whether it was the person in the line in front of us talking on the phone, the songs playing over the speakers, adverts over the airways or anything else he had heard while we were out. Over and over again, he would repeat these one-liners, often using them in response to my questions or to interrupt my conversations. Leaving the house became the hardest thing for me because I would often just return tired, Jordan covered in hives repeating one liners from people's conversations, new obsessions and allergic reactions.

There are things that your kids do that drive you crazy, and that's just part of normal funny everyday parenting! This one drove me mad! One day while I was trying to put him down for a nap, he noticed that the door to his bedroom made a kind of creaking sound when I shut it behind me. To him, it was new and interesting, which made him really happy and not sleepy at all. In fact, it produced the opposite effect, so when I heard him not sleeping, I would go back in and calm him down and tell him to sleep again. I would leave the room and the door would shut with another creaking noise, and again he was up and kicking.

This went on a few times before I refused to go back in, but we eventually had to bypass nap time altogether. However, it was already too late. He had found another obsession: he had adopted the door creaking sound as his favorite thing to do. He would wake up early in the morning and all he wanted to do was open and slam the door shut, all day long, every day. He ended up opening and slamming shut doors everywhere he was, continually, every three to five seconds for the next year or so. It didn't matter what door it was, where he was, a bathroom stall door, a cupboard or the front door to our apartment.. if it creaked, he would open it repeatedly. After a few weeks, I was simply done. No matter how many times I told him to stop or ran to stop him from doing it, he never listened and just went to slam another door in the house instead.

I nearly took all the doors off their hinges or attacked every one with a can of WD40! For that reason, it was really hard to go to public bathrooms, stores, other people's houses and churches, anywhere that had doors, really!

I had to physically restrain him all day long, holding him back from doing it repeatedly all the time. He was getting strong, and I couldn't hold him back and I didn't want to spend my whole time out holding him back. Discipline didn't work at all because he just didn't understand or notice anything I tried to teach him. In the end that obsession took around 4 years to break him free from.

People would ask me why I held onto him all the time, or why I holding him back. I tried to explain to them, but they had no grid for what was my daily normal. They had no idea what his obsessive tendencies were like or what it was like to deal with them. They had no idea how much work it took just to walk from the car to the house or store. They had no grid for what our lives were like. Partly due to my absolute exhaustion and other physical issues, the pain of the judgment and rejection that I would feel when I was out only added to the loneliness I struggled with. The house ended up being both a refuge and a prison for me. The strange combination of the silence of Jordan ignoring me all day intermingled with the intermittent babbling sounds that he made while he paced up and down talking to himself or slamming the doors was my normal now. This was now my life. I thought that if he was ignoring me, anyway, I might as well get busy with housework or reading or studying. But I discovered that it would irritate him if I walked away.

I would try to talk to him or play with him, but that would not last long before his inner world pulled him back and away from me. I would then walk away to get something done in the house, he would get mad and come and get me. He would start walking in circles in front of me and have me watch him. I didn't like being ignored or being made to watch his strange behavior sessions, because it was disconnecting for me to watch. When I did try to talk to him and break up his behavior patterns, try to have him connect with me in some way but every time I tried he would scream at me. I would have to sit there and listen to his strange talk and observe him rocking himself back and forth or opening and closing every door in the house, repeatedly.

When I had to sit there watching, I would dream of the everyday skills that average people take for granted. I would imagine playing happily with my child, talking to him and having him listen and talk back to me, and walking down a path holding hands.

Visions of talking to friends while our children played, eating regular food in a normal restaurant, or being able to to drink a cup of coffee in a café filled my thoughts. I didn't tell many people what was happening in our lives because they just didn't understand me when I explained it to them. Often I thought that they thought I was making up the details and that I was going through a depression. They would often just say "welcome to parenting." But I wasn't parenting really, nothing of what I was doing was normal or seemed like normal parenting. So I kept most of it to myself and stayed at home, hoping that one day it would be different.

For all Jordan's supposed checking out of life somewhere along the line he had lost a desire to connect with people nearly completely. After all, how do you make someone *want* to live his life and interact with others? You just cant.. From what I had seen and experienced, Jordan neither wanted to interact with the world nor noticed when I tried to teach him anything. He didn't want to do anything other than walk in circles, flapping his arms and talking to himself or watching T.V. He didn't want to feed himself or have any desire to grow up and learn. How do you encourage someone to want to grow up and learn or live and make them engage their life when they don't want to?

When I did see rays of hope where he had grasped a skill, such as a change in the way he walked or if he started to look at us in the eye a little more, it would often disappear the next day, leaving me hungry for growth and change. To see a change that was so needed in him and then have it disappear was the hardest thing to get used to. It is one of the classic Autistic characteristics, where they grasp a skill and then spend the day using it only to wake up the next day and its gone from their skill bank and memory. He would regress like an elastic band pulling back into place, sometimes worse than before. I think the struggle between progress and regress was the most painful thing I experienced because it rocks your trust in someone every day.

I started to see that I was responsible for a lot more than what I felt I could handle. It was as though I had taken on being his central processing unit. It was now my job to remind him to walk with his head straight and look forward instead of flipping his head all ways and forgetting to pick one foot up and place it in front of the other.

The very basic skills he had forgotten or not cared about. I had to get used to nagging him and constantly reminding him to chew his food and then swallow. For his own safety, every few seconds I had to tell him that he could breathe through his nose while he ate instead of screaming for air, or that he could walk with one foot in front of the other while looking at where he was going. I never thought I would have to be reminding/nagging him at every minute of every day how to swallow or breathe, but I did.

I also became his constant voice of reason and conscience, too. I would tell him that banging his head against a wall when he didn't get what he wanted was not a good idea. I would put myself in between him and the wall to protect him and that made me also become his bodyguard. I found that I also had become the translator for him. I would help him listen and translate for him when others tried to talk to him, and he would babble back a sentence that didn't make any sense, like a line from the TV show *Dora* or a conversation he had overheard.

I had been drafted for a job that I had not signed up for, yet here I was talking for him, translating for him, walking and moving his legs for him, carrying him, holding him, feeding him, being his memory and his conscience, massaging him, and being ignored by him. I protected him from allergies and food that made him sick and held his legs still so he could sleep and his eyelids shut when he needed a nap. And that when I looked at what our lives had become and felt exhausted. At the end of the day, I would end up going to bed every night crying and dreading the next day and what it would and wouldn't bring. What new challenges or obsessions would I find greeting me in the morning? This cycle was endless. I kept praying for a breakthrough and wondering when it would come.

Chapter 4

Enough

I came to the realization that every day was going to be a mystery to me now. When I woke up, I wouldn't know whether Jordan was going to be talking to me or screaming at me, if he would remember how to eat and chew or if I would have to spend the day re-teaching him again. How many allergic reactions was he going to have that day? And how far back would he regress from the previous day? Would he remember how to walk without tripping, or would he be able to walk beside me?

I dreamed that I would find a normal little boy smiling at me in the morning, looking in my eyes, engaging in conversation and laughing. Instead, it would always be the same strange silence, distant stares. I didn't feel like I was a normal mother or even a good mother at that. No matter what I did, Jordan was never happy with anything or the way I did it. I was constantly stressed out and sensitive to everything until it got to the point that I felt I had twisted and bent my life and world around to accommodate his little tendencies or needs. He refused to engage in life, grow and learn, and there was nothing I could do about it.

I had to find the balance between the challenge of getting him to grow and engage in life and the place where I would gently serve him and love on him. I found that most days one or both of us were crying and unhappy, and I wondered if or when we would enjoy life again.

One day I just cracked— but in a good way! I made the hard decision to challenge him. Something I had not really thought about before because I was only in survival mode.

This time I was not going to do what he wanted, when he wanted it, all the time. I was done doing everything for him because I was only getting more tired. I had not realized how much I was doing for him all the time. I was his constant reminder to eat, sleep, walk, talk, and breathe chew, pee, speak, listen or stop. That day I woke up tired of living in fear of upsetting him if I didn't do what he wanted all the time. I had had enough. I came to the realization one day that I was not supposed to live his life for him while he watched, and that it was not my soul job in life to make him constantly happy, all day, every day. I could not emotionally do it much longer without running completely dry myself. I asked God what I could do because I felt like what I was doing was not helping him. The Lord challenged me not to live in fear of my son's tantrums, not to bow to his every need and to allow Jordan to make mistakes. He said not to let the fear of man rule my parenting with him. I guess at some point, I had been so twisted and bent on making him happy that I listened to fear and let that guide me rather than Holy Spirit.

I began to use slow gentle reminders to let him figure things out for himself. Instead of me doing it all immediately for him, I felt like I had to now just relax a little more and allow him to begin to manage his world. I started letting him fall over his feet instead of me placing one in front of the other and helping him walk down a path. Instead of carrying him or holding him back from running, or helping him walk slowly while positioning his head to see where he was going, I allowed him to navigate his body instead. There were a few scraped knees and a lot of him screaming at me for not doing it for him or his tantrums at me for not protecting him from walking into a wall!

I let him drop his food on the floor, so that he would learn that if he was hungry enough to eat, then he would try to concentrate harder and get the food in his mouth. I gave him time to practice feeding himself instead of me re-teaching him every meal how to eat with a spoon or simply doing it for him all the time. There were basic survival skills that he had no idea how to tap into, himself. It was not like I hadn't tried to teach him. I had spent hours training him every day, but he always had me to rely on to do everything for him.

The things that the average person takes for granted, like when you are cold, you put a sweater on, etc., were difficult for him. He would be freezing and shivering, jumping hyperactively to warm himself up while a sweater was sitting right beside him. I would try to put the sweater on him, but he would cry and scratch at it, he couldn't handle the feeling of clothing sometimes. He knew how to put a sweater on, but he also couldn't see it so I had to point it out, ask him what it was, and what he should do with it? Often if he was hungry and food was right in front of him, he wouldn't pick it up and eat. He was too distracted to feed himself. In the rare occasion he saw it, he would either shove the whole thing in his mouth and cause himself to choke, or get too distracted to follow it through to his mouth from the plate. I had to let him figure out that the hunger would drive him to seek food out and find it waiting in front of him and therefore reach out to the food and place it in his mouth. Chew, breathe and swallow and repeat.

I challenged him to look in my eyes if he wanted something instead of screaming, while he stared at the wall or floor. If he wanted a snack or an electronic toy, I waited until he looked me in the eyes and asked me. If he screamed and hit me or bit me, he wouldn't get what he wanted until he calmed down. Instead of him rocking back and forth to comfort himself, I massaged him and sang to him while rocking him. Instead of him walking in circles, talking to himself, I stood in his path, so he could not get past me. I would then walk with him, in a straight line, talking to him instead.

Jordan didn't know how to respond to these changes. He was rather annoyed at first that I was not doing everything for him and cleaning up all the time. From my point of view I thought that I had taken on too much responsibility and it was time for him to have some back. I didn't see much change initially, which made it hard for me to continue, but my goal was to have a healthy normal son who could interact with the world and take care of himself.

In the middle of these new techniques one day I was getting so frustrated at the lack of progress, and screaming fits, that I sat down and asked God if he had any new ideas to get a breakthrough or facilitate a change in Jordan's behavior.

God said, "Copy him!" At first, I didn't think I was hearing the Lord correctly and thought I had imagined it. Then, I heard the Lord tell me again to mimic Jordan's behavior. It seemed childish and silly. Honestly, it didn't seem to be very mature for me to do everything he was doing, but I thought that it was worth a try.

There was plenty of opportunity to try this out on him, so one afternoon the usual thing happened where he wanted something and he motioned to me for it, expecting me to read his mind and get it for him. But this time I didn't, I wanted him to use the words I knew he could use. I turned around to ask him if he wanted something to drink but he made some strange sounds with his mouth while staring at the wall in response. Again, I asked him if he wanted something to drink and he did not acknowledge my question. Instead he ignored me while walking in circles, talking to himself. I remembered how God had said to copy him. So, I turned around and did what he was doing. I ignored him, while walking in a circle, talking to myself and flapping my hands up and down! He was shocked. He looked up at me with a puzzled face and stopped what he was doing. He said loudly, "NOOOO!" He spoke clearly as if he had no problems speaking. He stopped his strange behavior, came over to where I was, pulled me down to his level. With his little hands holding my face he clearly said, "STOP IT, MOMMY!" That was it...Bingo!

We were stuck in that moment, with my face in his hands and our eyes meeting. He realized that he was looking me in the eyes and it didn't hurt him, but as quickly as he seemed to come out of himself to connect, he pulled away again. For a few moments, I saw into his soul and spirit. I connected with his eyes, which was rare. I knew then that somewhere deep inside he was in there alive, awake and able to respond, but something was holding him back. It was amazing to me that all along he was aware of what he was doing and didn't seem to want to stop his behavior. What God told me to do worked! (What a surprise that God was right all along!) It was not mature or dignified or pretty to watch, but I got my point across. It showed him what he looked like and opened his eyes to his own behavior.

Chapter 5

Time for a Change

Not only did parenting strain our bodies and our friendships but it started to really weigh on my relationship with God. I had no time to be with him, read my Bible, pray, talk or worship. I couldn't go to church because of Jordan's food, and his environmental allergies were still bad and the noise of the music would over stimulate his sensory system. It was just easier to stay at home. At least at home I could take whatever time I could and talk to God, whether it was doing the washing up, cleaning up the house or enjoying the silence when Jordan had finally gotten to sleep. Although it was not always quality time, it was often all a mother could do and I know that God understood that.

It changed my prayer life because your prayer life comes out of who you think you are in God and what place you are in your relationship with God. Mine was in a desperate state, a place where I was barely surviving, so that made my prayers desperate, short and demanding. I think that deep down I was a little angry at him for letting this all happen to us. I prayed in any case desperate prayers, repetitive prayers. Any free minute I had I cried out to God for help for a response from heaven, anything. Why was God not answering me? Had I done something to make this happen? The Bible says that his grace is sufficient, but it sure didn't feel like it most days. There was a huge conflict in my mind going on.

I was desperate for help but didn't know where to turn. I was in a new country and had moved here for my husband's job. I had no family around and limited friends. But I had never seen anything like this before or been around kids who acted like this. This strange behavior had become my normal, being ignored or screamed at, the tantrums or fits of being over stimulated were my daily visitors.

It was only when I went out and saw how other kids acted that I realized that Jordan's behavior was not normal, and it became increasingly clear that my child was different from the others. It sounds horrible to say out loud, but sometimes I would see the other kids and their families and wish that I had their life just for a day or two.

One day when Jordan was nearly two, while I was chatting with my landlady in front of my house and our kids were playing together in the driveway, she started to look at Jordan and she got that familiar look on her face. I knew that look, as if she was wandering if there was something different or wrong with Jordan. I thought, "Oh great. Here we go again. Someone else we won't be able to spend time with because she thinks there's something wrong with my child," and I braced myself for rejection. She said, "You know, I had my son evaluated by something called 'early intervention' for speech therapy. You should give them a call; they might be able to help you. They gave him speech therapy twice a week in our home, which helped him just to catch up." At first, I was slightly insulted. I mean we were standing around talking about something completely different when out of the blue she points something out in my son. I was polite when I thanked her for her suggestion and when we finished talking I went inside the house and thought about what she said. I did not put two and two together for a while because I was still upset at yet another person pointing out something in my son. But after I thought it some more, I remembered that I had asked God for help. Yet when it came in a different form from what I expected, I was too hurt to see it clearly. If I could just see past my own pride and not let offense hinder me, I could receive the help I desperately needed. I called my landlady back and asked her for their number. I had never heard of anything like this before, but I was willing to give it a try. I didn't know if it really was just me imagining all the odd behaviors or if Jordan truly needed help that I could not provide him. I called and set up an appointment for the following week. I was nervous, yet I knew that I needed to face this thing and see what could be done to help my son.

The day came when I heard their knock at the front door. I opened it, and a team of smiling therapists' faces met me. They introduced themselves one by one as they came in and made themselves comfortable in my living room.

With them they had brought piles of paperwork and forms to fill out, suitcases filled with toys, and hope in their eyes. Jordan just stared from the other corner of the room. He was never rude to people who came over, but he was wondering what was in the huge suitcases lying in between him and the big people staring at him. One by one, they played with him, pulling out tons of toys and watching to see how he would react and how he would play. They talked to him, tested him and scribbled furiously on their clipboards. I sat there watching them, answering the many questions posed at me, and filling out all the forms handed to me. When it was all over, they picked up their things, thanked me for the call, said good-bye to Jordan and left. They seemed really nice and eager to help me, but I was scared and left wondering whether I was going to get help or be alone.

I was dreading the results, what if they thought that I had caused this to happen or had made him sick in some way? I was a little nervous when I got the call a few days later. They had come to a decision and we needed to meet. I arranged a meeting with our caseworker for the following week and when she came in, she explained what I already knew deep down. They saw that he needed some help and that they wanted to help by setting up a team of therapists to get him all he needed. I was not alone anymore. They all pulled out their calendars and started marking off dates and fitting him into their schedules. And before five minutes was up, we had eight sessions a week planned out with other days too for group play dates. As they talked about it all with each other swapping calendars, I silently breathed a sigh of relief and on the inside I cried.

The pediatrician also suggested that we have him evaluated by a neurologist. The word "neurologist" alone just plain overwhelmed me. I associated that word with brain tumors or brain surgery, not something like this. But I made an appointment anyway. He had an evaluation with the doctor and had an MRI and an EEG done as well. She evaluated and tested him and eventually told us what I had already known deep in my heart, so when she gave the diagnosis, I wasn't shocked: "autism." It wasn't a really severe case, but a medium one.

While he had all the usual character traits that were on the spectrum of disorders, he also had some great social skills but had no desire to use them. So our main goal was to focus on the daily therapy and get him motivated to come out of his shell and interact with us all.

Honestly, the diagnosis didn't bother me. I didn't hear those words and shudder or cry. I just nodded my head. I had shut down to a certain degree and was just dealing with all the general day-to-day struggles of handling Jordan and was not so much bothered with the diagnosis. But this was the first time I had ever really been confronted with this kind of thing. It rocked my stability and altered all I thought would fit into a "normal" range of life. This is something that you can never or should never prepare for when you are pregnant or thinking about becoming a parent. When something like this hits your life, it never sits well in your heart, neither is it something you can settle into or get used to. It wasn't something that I had grown up knowing anything about or was around, so my meter for childhood problems was set at zero. After the doctor gave us her opinion, it made me start thinking that this was not an end of a journey, but the beginning of one. It never crossed my mind that he would not improve, even though I had only ever seen him regress and progress and regress again. To me it was a matter of WHEN he was going to be normal and not IF.

Meanwhile at home, the therapy had already started, and I sat every day watching from the corner of our living room. I marveled at how they worked with him, he instantly responded to them and opened up for them in ways he never opened up for me. For hours I observed how they talked to him, what they watched for in his response, what they were looking for in his behavior, and what they wanted him to do. Just by their being in the house and seeing him every day he had already started to improve. Although I obviously needed a break from things, it was more important for me to sit and watch their techniques and learn from them than to do something else around the house or nap even!! It was like a glorified play session for him, something that I had, no matter how many times I tried, not been able to get him to do with me. Children learn through play and it's the start of their learning career.

For whatever reason, he opened right up and played with them really well. He, of course, liked being the center of attention, and that made the therapy easier for him. For them he would play and learn. But everything that I had tried to do for so long and had failed at, was now working when they walked in and started to play with him. They had a magic touch, it seemed.

Day after day and week after week, they kept plodding away and working with him. They were amazing to watch, and I learnt so much from them. I used their techniques in the everyday life situations that arose and in general with my son to keep the continuity of therapy going. It was just plain good parenting techniques mixed with good teaching skills. The hardest thing for me was that when they left, he would revert straight back to screaming at me, forgetting how to talk, and not wanting to play with toys or interact with me. I seemed to bring out a side of his character that not a lot of people saw or could handle. They saw a side of him that was amazing and saw incredible breakthroughs and changes, while I, on the other hand, saw the regress and the struggle, the anger and the tantrums from the moment the front door was closed behind them. No one wants to bring out the worst in their children. I got very frustrated that I didn't have the magic touch to make this all go away.

The truth was I wanted there to be a magic wand that when waved over him would eliminate all the hardships, and then I would have a normal, happy, healthy child. I wanted to not be ignored, I wanted to be talked to, to have him play with me with toys, to be able to walk into a store peacefully or play in a park with other kids, have play dates, go to church, and travel. That had always seemed so far away but I didn't want to give up my dreams just yet.

They were the best team anyone could ask for. It felt like God had handpicked them especially for Jordan, and he certainly loved seeing them every day. With them, he blossomed and took great strides, but with me, he still struggled with progress and regress. If they had not come along when they did, there is no telling where we would be today.

Chapter 6

The question

A year had passed since we started early intervention therapy. Although he continued to have daily allergic reactions to things and his hyperactivity was a constant struggle, he was making small steps with the things we worked on every day. His speech was still at the same level, and his eye contact was limited, but he developed a love for people that was unusual for classic autistic children. Past his love and desire to be with people, he would always hit a wall with his limited social skills. He wanted to be around other children, but had no idea what was appropriate behavior or speech around them, often flapping his arms and repetitive behavior and other classic autistic behavior. It would often scare the other children or overwhelm them so they wouldn't want to play with him.

One day I think I must have had a hard week because I remember sitting down and telling God that I thought that this whole thing was not fair. It seemed just not right that this sort of thing existed on earth at all and that there was no solution for it. I asked Him why it was taking so long to see anything change in our lives, why it was taking God so long to answer one simple request.
I was doing everything I could, I had changed my life around, the house upside down, therapy every day, I had no life past the four walls, yet no reply from heaven. In my eyes, this whole thing had pushed me farther away from God and that hurt probably just as much, if not more, than anything else. That was when the big question came. You know, the one that started this whole book...

"Liz, would you stay with me if I never healed your son?"

As I said I was having one my "THOSE" days that all mothers have once in a while. I was tired from repeating myself, tired from not sleeping, tired from being ignored, tired from the therapy, and tired from housework. Hopelessness seemed to follow me around that day like a whining puppy that I would keep tripping over and I had had enough. I was already crying as I walked down the hallway when I heard the Lord ask me that question. Somewhere between the bedroom and the living room, with the laundry basket in my hand, God caught me off guard by asking me a question. My first thought was: "Where have you been? Why have you not been talking to me this whole time?" But the truth is, to hear God's voice in the middle of your valley of death, whether it is a whole sermon or one word is better than ice cold water in 110-degree heat. I was just so happy to hear his lovely voice that it overwhelmed me as much as the question itself.

I dropped everything I was doing and just fell to the floor in a puddle of tears. With all the tiredness and the emotional strain, that question completely caught me off guard. I ran through the possible scenarios of what life might be like for us all if things didn't get better, and at that thought I lost hope for my situation. I was a wimp because I honestly thought that I could not handle another day of this, let alone a lifetime of long-term care. I just couldn't do this all anymore without the hope of healing. But I could not understand how God could ask me that kind of a question at a time like that; it just didn't seem fair at all.

So I got a little angry and answered him with, "What do you mean? How am I supposed to carry on this way for the rest of my life? I didn't ask for this. This is already too hard for me. And now you ask me this—*YOU*, who made the heavens and the earth—ask me to keep things the way they are and you don't lift a finger to change my son's life."

In the middle of my tantrum and mess, in the middle of the forced obsessive cleaning and extreme diet control, I had to make a decision. And it was easy, yet hard at the same time. What was I going to choose? I had known the Lord for as long as I could remember. I remember his voice and seeing him when I was a young child. I remember his presence with me always, and I could not look back at my life and not see him in every single day, nor could I imagine a day without him being in my life.

But I took a good look at what my life had become. It was desolate and desperate and tiring to survive and I didn't know if I could carry on one more hour, let alone a lifetime. And now I had to choose. God had slipped down from his number one spot, the place where he had always been, to a close second. Being a mother and a wife would naturally mean that things would change, and I knew I would have to juggle my attention and devotion, but this was something different. I felt like I was a slave to this thing that was robbing our child of life. I felt like I was in prison, held captive to my son's every emotional, physical, and medical need. I had realized that my desire for my son's healing to manifest in our lives had taken over the importance of relationship with the King of Kings.

I realized from the evidence of my stinky tantrum that I was selectively hearing one part of the question and not hearing the whole of it. I had only heard *"If I never heal your son"*! But that wasn't all that he was saying. God wanted to know if I was willing to stay with him, if things got bad, ugly, hard, lonely, even harder still and if he never did anything for me again. Was I willing to pick him over the benefits of knowing the almighty powerful strong miracle working Father? Was I in this relationship for him or for what I could get out of him?

After I calmed down and took a deep breath, I took a look at *why* I reacted the way I did to the question. My interpretation and reaction to the question was that things weren't going to change for us. I already felt abandoned and isolated as it was. The prospect of living in that place for a lifetime with not enough God and surviving autism was daunting to me. I thought that he was only going to give me a little of Him and have the big, ugly autism stay lodged in our lives and cause us all pain and separation. It took me a while to think about it all, but I came to the conclusion that without God, life would be hell. With God, it was bliss. Simple. That question had in fact changed my life.

So I spent a while looking at my heart. What I found wasn't that pretty and I needed to shift my thinking and my love for God. After a while I went back to the Lord later, knelt down and said, "Absolutely, I would stay with you, no matter what." And that was it. I had moved from a servant like relationship to a covenant.

Because of that change in my relationship with him, my prayer life needed to change, too. Until that time, honestly, I was just nagging him and not really praying. You have to examine your heart when you pray. It's from there that you speak to him. If your heart is bitter, distant, in pain, angry even, then you often pray from that place. But mostly you pray according to who you think you are to him or how he sees you.

It seemed to me after that question was posed that I was either praying with the wrong motives or in the wrong way. I was praying from who I thought I was and not who God said I was. I thought that I didn't mean that much to him, that I needed to strive or fight for everything and that if anything needed to be done, I would have to do it myself. I thought I needed to work for God's love, that this healing would come if I nagged (and by nag I mean pray) him enough. But, if I did anything wrong then he wouldn't give it to me.

It exposed what I thought of him as a Father and exposed me as an orphan. It was actually my identity as his daughter that God wanted to deal with that day he asked me the question. It was not so much about my son's healing, although that was important to him and me but about where I was as a child. That was going to be a lot of work and not a quick fix. I had let this orphan mindset live in my life for too long, and although my son needed help and my prayers, I realized that God wanted me to see myself properly and get healed first.

After I answered him with my "Absolutely I would stay with you no matter what," things didn't really change. You might be thinking *what was the point then*? But my goal and expectations had shifted. I wasn't thinking of what I could get out of God but where I was with God. So things carried on as normal, the therapy, the tantrums, the hyperactivity and the allergic reactions. But my heart was a little more at peace now.

One afternoon a few months later I examined my heart and thought I would really like to pray differently and feel like I'm not nagging God. So I asked him, "Okay, God, I know you hear me. I want to pray your prayers and pray from your heart, with your view and using your words. I want to know what exactly you want me to do now and how you want me to pray, please. Amen."

I felt him smiling at me, as if he had been waiting for me to come to that point where I had given up my way of doing things.

I heard him ask gently, "What do you want Liz?"

I stopped what I was doing and replied, "I want to see this 'thing' gone. I want to understand this 'thing' from your point of view. I want more of you. I want to see the results from my prayers. I want my son back, and I want to see other children set free from this. Please give me the knowledge of a seasoned special needs therapist, an occupational therapist, a speech therapist, and a psychologist. I also need the insight of a neurologist so I can see into his brain functions and know what to pray for. I want my eyes to be open to see what is really going on inside my son, even down to the molecular level, so I can see this thing for what it is. Let's come up with a plan of action and start rebuilding him from the inside out. Also, I want you to give me more wisdom and more insight and understanding because I have had enough of my view of this thing and now I want yours, Father. Amen."

"Okay." He simply said, while smiling at me. And once again that was all the Lord said to me. (God likes to give me one-word answers.) I felt like God was up to something and that he had been waiting for me to get to that point where I could not do it anymore on my own. That night I went to bed wondering what God was up to! I mean he is always up to something, but in this case, I wondered what his one word answer meant and what to expect next.

It was in those first few glorious moments when I woke up the next morning, that I realized something had either been added to my mind or had been unblocked. I could not describe it well, but all I knew was that as I got up and started taking care of my son, something was different. I could not put my finger on it or describe it perfectly, but my mind was different than the day before. I had a day scheduled full of therapy sessions, and when the therapists knocked on the front door and came in, I felt the usual sense of relief as they started working with Jordan.

I settled into my usual spot sitting in the corner of the room watching and began praying for them as they plodded away at the training. I had been observing them for months. Only this time, I understood what they were doing and why. This morning, instead of praying random prayers of desperation, mixed with expectations and frustration through the hours of therapy, I could start to feel God's Spirit of revelation flow through my mind. God was up to something in my head.

That morning something had changed, and all I can say is that I finally got it. My vision connected to the spirit of revelation, and as I "read" my son's body, I saw him struggling with things they were trying to teach him. I saw into his body, saw for example how his muscles were tight and why. So from there I prayed instead. I had a renewed vision and purpose. Praying from that point was way more fun than struggling prayers like, "Oh, God, do something! His muscles aren't working. Come on Father, can't you see he needs help?" That was the best day of therapy we had had so far.

Something about my brain was different that morning. I felt like God had given me a new pair of eyes that saw into Jordan's life, his body and soul in more detail. And from there I turned what I saw into prayer and intercession. It was a whole new different feeling to partner with God than nag him. I could feel God smile back at me as I prayed about the things he needed. And that in turn made me smile, too.

Chapter 7

Changing my identity, changing my prayers

"If we rejoice in the acts of God without discovering His ways, we'll question who He is when He doesn't do what we've asked." Bill Johnson

I thought that God had given me this hard situation because I had done something wrong, and that I also deserved to be punished. That this situation happening to me was because of my messing up in life, a sort of pay back for my sins. I could not be further from the truth. Father God knew perfectly well what I thought of him, he knew what my view of the situation was and also knew where my prayers were based from. The old mindset wasn't working, nor was the frustration coming through my prayers. Something needed to change, but I didn't really know what. I had always prayed that way, thinking that I could make God do what I wanted him to.

Before, I had treated my times with him in prayer like a lawyer, feeling like I had to defend my case to a mean judge. That wrong view of him I can imagine, must have cut deeply into his heart. I could not have been more wrong about him. He is so loving. There needed to be an exchange of lies for the truth. He would never barge his way into our mind or life and demand that we see him for who he truly is, defending himself against the lies that we have often agreed with. The truth is he is constantly good and loving. He doesn't and cannot change who he is.

He cannot nor will he bend or mould to fit our view of him, especially when it is so wrong and goes against truth. But he does want to walk beside us and help us sort through, separating the lies from the truth, so we can see him for who he truly is. The only truth is, he is eternally good and pure, holy, loving and caring. And he is a good father and no amount of lies will ever change that.

Can God trust his kingdom into the hands of orphans? No. It was meant for adopted children who know the heart of God, who understand what the kingdom of God look likes and how it works. Because an orphan only knows that love (or love they experience) usually comes with bad side effects (guilt, control, distrust anyone, fear of man, people pleasing, or service for love). Every child of God needs to have a love encounter with him, and needs to get a revelation of his love for them to be able to represent him well. Orphans pray, walk, talk and think differently from adopted children. They have one eye always at their back always ready to bolt when things get hard.

He wanted to change my identity before I could change the way I prayed. I discovered repeating myself, or using fancy long-winded prayers, when I secretly thought he was a hard-hearted father, didn't actually move God's heart. You can't fool him! I would pray these long prayers and use elaborate language or even get smart and quote Bible verses at him. But at the end of the day, more words are sometimes just more. The Bible says, "Out of the heart, the mouth speaks" (Matthew 12:34). Out of my life and who I think I am to God, do I speak my prayers.

The revelation of how I was thinking hit me straight between the eyes. I needed to change my view of him and his love, and remove all the lies from our relationship for us to be closer. When my identity changed, my relationship changed and when our relationship changed my prayers changed. So I needed a dismantling of the old mind and an installation of the new adopted child mind instead! When I saw myself and God from his perspective, I found that my thoughts towards the Father and indeed towards myself were drastically wrong in every way. I didn't know how to pray after that revelation. Before I guess I was whining and had gotten used to praying that way. After he lovingly showed me how much he loved me, then I was tongued tied as to what to pray.

I would sit down to pray or start to say something and then freeze! I didn't know what to say next. I somehow couldn't get past the " Dear Father" part and often just parked there. Eventually I decided that the one prayer Jesus took time to teach us, the Lords Prayer, was probably the safest place to start. And that first line "My father..." is the ideal place to start from when the orphan mindset has been dismantled in your life.

" My father in heaven... Lord let your kingdom come, let your will be done." So we just went over and over that prayer. Every line was like a meal and had life all over it. I declared that the Father's will be done in my son's life, here on earth, as the King's dominion is carried out in heaven. You can't have one without the other. You cannot see King Jesus and not see his kingdom, which is an extension and example of his goodness. When we say, "Your kingdom come and your will be done, on earth as it is in heaven," heaven's kingdom becomes superimposed over earth. All of God's goodness is overlaid over my world. That prayer is fuel or a power meal! Everything you need is in that one prayer. Jesus knew what he was doing when he showed us how to pray that prayer. If you need to start somewhere in your prayers and don't know what to say, may I suggest you always start there?

I know that there is no mental illness in heaven, no missing limbs, or paralyzed people up there being wheeled around. There is no depression and no autism, either. If there is none in heaven, then Jesus' crucifixion and resurrection provided a way for there to be none down here. Jesus taught us how to pray in Luke 11:2: "Our Father in heaven, hallowed be your name." This is the biggest confrontation to the orphan mindset. My Father in heaven. *"My Father."* It's that important to him that we grasp who we are and pray from that place. Luke 2:1 continues, "Your kingdom come, your will be done, on earth as it is in heaven." The kingdom is not filled with orphans, but with adopted, loved, and belonging children. The kingdom is filled with love and children who know their father.

I felt like I partnered with God when I prayed then and I could see his smile on his face when I started to pray differently. I coupled the new identity I had grasped and was living out along with the revelations and new sight into Jordan's therapy.

From then on, I therefore prayed over every bit of odd behavior I saw come up in Jordan, I declared "Your kingdom come, your will be done in my son's life, in his body as your will is done in heaven." If I saw that he was lacking in something or not coping well in a situation, I then prayed in what he needed to deal with it.

Instead of focusing on what he was lacking or using fear to fuel prayer, I prayed in what he lacked and released love. Instead of just seeing a strange character trait or sensory need and battling with it, I decided that I was going to now use my words in prayer to create the things Jordan was missing in his life.

When my son was restless and on edge, I prayed for peace. In places he needed coordination, I prayed over his head so that his brain would talk to his body with ease and that his neurons would talk to each other properly, I declared life over his brain, over his body.

One day, after a frustrating day of working with my son, I just collapsed on the couch. It was one of those days where nothing was working in therapy and I had run out of strength emotionally and physically. As I sat down on the couch I looked out the window and cried out for help. I asked Him why the healing for the mind seemed harder to get than if someone was to be healed of something else such as an infection. Why are some people so well adjusted and others struggle with basic everyday tasks such as eating, walking or going to the bathroom?

I was complaining at how frustrating it was just to get Jordan to walk and feed himself when everyone else's child seems to know what to do instictively. Why was there such a great divide between mental illness and the seemingly normal ones. I could feel God come up close to me and whisper very gently in my ear, "Lizzie, you are ALL mentally disabled compared to me, and without me, you are incomplete." I started laughing so hard that I nearly fell off the couch. I had judged my son harshly, thinking that I was better than he was. Somehow, I thought I was more together and normal than he was! I was sitting there comparing him to my *great wholeness* (sarcasm intended!) and being hard on him for not matching up to other's standards, when God opened my eyes to see that we were not so different after all. That simple and life challenging truth from the Father's mouth put all of my son's and my problems into perspective.

We think that some appear to be more normal than others and that God uses the "normal ones" because they are better than you or me. In reality, God sees us all as the same. It's not a ladder where Billy Graham is at the top and others are way at the bottom, among the kooky, different ones. There are no class and sub classes with him. God doesn't have super popular and wonderful people molds on the special top shelf of his creation cabinet, and then have the everyday John and Jane Doe on the bottom shelf. People with limbs missing, minds not whole, stuck in a rut, famous in Hollywood, millionaires, are all the same to him. All are wanted, called by name, loved eternally, and created with care.

Jesus died not just for some healings. He didn't leave out some that were resistant to the power of his blood. He didn't die only for all the diseases that were known during the time he walked on earth, but also for all diseases and strains that they could ever mutate into. That includes mental illnesses or disabilities, deformities of the brain or body.

Once I saw we are all cherished and loved on an equal basis, and that any disease could be healed, I started feeling a whole lot better about my situation and capabilities. I felt like I exchanged my view of what needed to happen with all its faithless opinions for his. His view was that it was not all my responsibility, that it's all about his love, that he promised to give us a spirit of power, love and a sound mind. So I was going to take him at his word.

Chapter 8

Another question from God

God often chose to talk to me in the quiet moments when, on the rare occasion my son would take a nap! Not too many months after God had started to renew my mind, I was staring at the trees in the woods opposite my house just relaxing when I heard: "Fast or slow?"

"Huh?" I thought.

He asked again, "Do you want this to go the fast way or the slow way?"

I said, "Do You think you could be more specific? What do you mean fast or slow?"

"I am going to take you on a journey. The foundations of your life on which you have built are not good. The only way you can have the life you are supposed to have is if I took your house apart and broke up the foundation stones and rebuilt you. It is going be painful, so you can go the slow way or the fast way. Which one do you want to do?" he asked again.

"Oh, okay. Thanks for telling me." I replied, (with a slight sarcastic tone!).

"You did ask me to change your life and your son's!" He replied with the equal amount of honesty and wit.

"I know, I know. But I was thinking that you could do it kinda like Adam with the rib. You know, put me to sleep and wake me up when it's all done, bada bing, bada boom!" I replied hoping he would listen to my wit.

"Do you want it the fast way or the slow way?" he asked. I could tell He desired an honest answer and no more dodging his question with my sarcasm.

"I see you didn't get my joke. Okay, hang on a minute." I ran through a few scenarios in my mind, imagining what the outcome would be like. Thinking it would be like a bandaid that you just have to rip off quickly.

"Okay, then, the fast way...like a band aid...rip it off quick. Do it the fast way, please.... Er, I think!. Hang on, wait. Did I choose the right way?.. Wait."

"Okay." He replied. And that was it.

Then it hit me. What did I just agree to? Why wasn't there a third option there? I thought my suggestion of Adam and the rib thing was pretty good! What was he going to do and more to the point, when?

I could not have a healed son and not be healed, myself. It came as a package deal, heal one, get the other free kinda thing. I knew as the authority over my son's life, if I did not allow God to do the same thing in me then the healing in my son could not fully go deep in him. I won't lie;I was nervous. When God offered me an option of slow and painful or fast and painful, I broke out in a cold sweat because in both options is the word "pain"! And when God says painful, He often means it!

That same day somewhere among the laundry loads and the therapy I had a vision. My view opened up to a dark, stormy sky. Kind of like Kansas when a twister is about to touch down, and the sky is black with clouds and wind. The moon illuminated a piece of land where an old house stood. The house looked like it was a shack that had been battered by the winds and weathered. It had a slant to it and was leaning to one side. Jesus walked onto the plot of land with some tools and a sledgehammer and started to tear it down. He looked like a man on a mission, and I could see his strength and resolve as he ripped planks of wood off this unlivable shack. He neither noticed the storm in the sky, and the wind rattling up against the loose planks of siding nor was put off by the task at hand.

He just went straight to business. Piece by piece, plank by plank, the house slowly came down. First the roofing, then the siding of the house, then the windows and doors came off. The bearing beams that held the walls up were left stark and standing alone. I heard thuds from a huge hammer thumping away and cracking wood as the structure lost its cohesion. Nothing was left but a few beams and a growing pile of discarded building materials off to one side of the demolished house. After a while, I saw Jesus walk back onto the piece of land with a pair of safety goggles and a huge sledgehammer. Again, he looked intent on his mission and I heard his voice say, "This is going to hurt, Liz." He started whacking with his full strength on the concrete foundation slab. Bang! Bang! Bang! What moved me was the loving tone in his voice when he told me, "It's going hurt, Liz." He was resolute and yet with every slamming thud you could hear his heartbeat.

Jesus loved me so much that he didn't want to leave me in the same mess as he found me. Tirelessly, he banged away without stopping for a break. Bit by bit, there appeared dents in the concrete. Chunks went flying, and I could feel the vibrations going through my soul. Just the vision of him working that hard brought me to tears, and I felt a shaking in the very core of me. Then the vision ended. And I was where I had been sitting, shaking and crying. What do you do after that? The only thing I could do was to kneel and thank him. That was the beginning of what was actually a season of God lovingly dismantling things in my life.

A few days later I was walking through my vegetable patch in the garden when God said to me very clearly, "Where would you like me to begin?" It's not that I thought I had gotten off the hook but I did think that maybe he was going to do it in my sleep or in a few months time, but he ambushed me in the strawberry patch! I thought about it for a while and said the first thing that came to mind: "I guess at the beginning...." It seemed logical to only begin at the beginning. Then right where I stood, in my mind, I was transported back to a time in my life when something horrible happened to me. I was watching this scene not from my view but looking on as it unfolded before my eyes. I had buried this memory deep down where I thought that I would never find it.

It was so strange to see because at first I was not sure if it was one of my memories, but after a few seconds of watching it, I started to remember details. It was as if someone had gone through the basement of my life and turned on all the lights and opened all the doors and windows and let the air in. I was almost winded when I saw it. I stopped in my tracks, allowed the memory to be viewed and started crying. That was the beginning of a series of events that were painful to watch. They certainly opened a door to something in my life, they started a ball rolling in how I was treated or seen. God started at one of the youngest most painful memories I had. I could not get away from it or find a place for it in my life so I was faced with sorting through this situation with him and offering it up to him and letting his love heal that memory.

That day he started something. Memory after memory, that I had repressed and kept secret, came up continuously for weeks. Sometimes he opened up whole years of my life, and I relived them, seeing different angles and seeing the missing parts. I was able to have some resolution as I cleared out the secret places of my life. Not a day went by without something coming up to see and deal with. I was emotionally exhausted and my diary became full of memories and the processes of healing them with God's help. Although he let me see it all, he never let me see it alone; he was always there in the middle of it.

One of the biggest things I had struggled with for years was depression. It was like an ongoing roller coaster of turmoil and pain that I just wanted to get away from but couldn't. I had no idea why I could not control my mood, control my emotions or settle down from extreme highs and devastating lows. I think God had needed to get at all those other memories to get the root of that ugly, unwanted depression. Those things had happened to me at such a young age and I had no way to deal with them in a healthy way so they stayed where I had stored them, unreconciled and causing more trouble for me. It had been the longest and loudest cry of my heart to have a breakthrough in my mind, to see this depression that ruled my life leave and to feel freedom once and for all.

I remember after a period of months and of having these memories resurface daily if not multiple times a day, I asked him to just take out the depression because I could no longer live with it.

I saw that all those memories and unhealthy thinking patterns were piled up on the waste heap waiting to be picked up and taken away. And I just wanted the garbage truck to come quickly and take it all away. So I simple prayed "Father please please take this depression away from me. I never want to see it again in my life." An amazing thing happened while I slept because the next morning I could literally and physically feel the change when I woke up. My eyes opened and I started my usual stressing out of what's going to happen today with Jordan? What time is therapy? What is on my housework list? When I stopped and noticed something was indeed missing from my brain. The heaviness was gone that I had been so used to. Like a weight that was always attached to my mind. I felt like someone had opened all the doors and windows in my brain, and now I could feel for the first time. The pure enjoyment of those first few moments of being awake was something I will never forget. The cloud that I had lived under wasn't hanging over my bed when I woke up. My chin was plastered to the floor in shock, and I laughed for the first hour after I woke up! I was smiling from ear to ear, and I enjoyed every minute of it. I kept saying, "There's something different, but I can't put my finger on it." For the first time in my life, I had clarity in my mind. It took a good few hours to fully get used to the experience of the freedom that was just released in my being. It wasn't just the feeling in my mind, but I honestly felt a chemical change in my body. Headaches and stress were gone, hunger for food was back, tastebuds were alive. That day for the first time in such a long time, I felt alive in every sense of the word, and I enjoyed every minute of it.

Breakthroughs in other areas that I had previously struggled with were suddenly happening, too. One of the areas that I had really had a hard time in was concentrating in school. Somehow the depression and fear made it very hard for me to concentrate at all or get anything done. When I was younger, I couldn't read very well or write either as a result of it. My head felt so cluttered all the time that I couldn't even read a sentence properly. I had a hard time reading anything at all.

I couldn't understand a word I was looking at, and a jumble of colors and numbers jumped out of the page and assaulted my eyes. I was hugely dyslexic and often read right to left, starting at the end of a page and moved upwards to the beginning of the text. I, in the end, barely skimmed my way through school.

After the depression left, the first thing I did was to grab a book and start to read. It was one of the ways I could know that my mind was free enough to comprehend anything. And to my shock, I finished a 700-page book in two days. My mind was coming alive! I had been told all my life that I was stupid and that I could not do anything right and I was starting to think that that actually was not true!

I had never been able to read a sentence without trouble, let alone an entire book cover to cover. Then a memory surfaced from my childhood. I must have been five years old when my mother asked me what I wanted to do when I grew up. I told her that I wanted to write books about God and to tell people about his character and started to write stories about his character and love on this cute little writing pad. Directly after that a lot of bad things happened, hindering me and causing a depression to settle in my mind. After that I could not read well, I could not write well and my school grades were not good. But in a matter of months God had ripped out the depression and had freed my mind.

God kept surprising me by freeing other areas in my mind after taking out the depression. When he started to heal my brain and take out the depression, I found that I actually thought differently. When I thought differently, I could use my mind as it was designed for, for life. And then I started to see properly. When I saw properly, I could start to display a hunger for understanding things and asking questions. Like the five-year-old with the endless number of questions, I turned into a question machine!! Questions are a healthy example of a hunger to understand more and grow up. Before, the sounds of the teachers and bullies yelling at me that I was too dumb resounded and decapitated all desires to learn and grow. Now without confusion or fear, I dared to ask God questions I had never even thought of before. It seemed I had some growing and catching up to do! So I started asking him how to do things, to show me how things were made. I wanted to understand science, math, gardening, sewing, knitting, and cooking. I wanted to succeed at everything that I could not do before.

It was more than reading and writing, it was cleaning the house, cooking, remembering things that I would have easily forgotten before. It was learning to live my life without fear or confusion anymore, and I liked the changes.

I no longer killed every houseplant given to me, (even the plastic ones). I started to ask God to teach me how to garden instead, as he was the first and best gardener that ever existed. I asked God for the best cooking tips, and my list became pages long. My dreams came alive, and so did the rest of my life.

As a result of that incredible breakthrough, my walk with God changed. He changed the foundations of who I was and started to rebuild me from the inside out. Who I was becoming, and my relationship with him deepened and slowly the old wounds were healing. Hunger for the word of God came back, where now I was able to read my Bible with freedom and without stress.

I started to get revelatory downloads on Scriptures, and in my dreams, I heard God talking to me and showing me things and more revelations. My spirit was coming alive, and I liked all that God was doing. In contrast to the pain of the previous months of ripping apart, this was like being at a bank and God handing me his debit card and telling me to go shopping for my heart's desires!

I looked back at how I was praying for my son, from the old me and the broken down house and those things that were clouding my vision of who God was. The depression wouldn't allow me to think properly. But the more I understood God and his heart for me, the more he healed me, and therefore the more effective my prayers became. The closer to his heart I got, the more I shared his vision for my circumstances, and my prayers changed. The old orphan mindset with all its ugliness had left. It had no place to live from now. In replacement was an adopted child who could see her Father God clearly for the first time.

Chapter 9

To bed, bath and beyond

Up until this point, my son had not changed much. God was doing more work in me it seemed while we plodded away at his daily therapy sessions and diet management. I was praying continually for him during this time but, thankfully, from a new mindset. I found it painful to be feeling so free in my life, yet seeing my son struggle with basic, everyday life. One moment while I was resting in between therapy sessions one day, I heard God say to me:

"What goes in, must come out, Liz."

I knew of the Newton Theory of physics of "What goes up, must come down," but I had not heard of this one before. He had a habit of always turning up and hitting me with a great "one-liner" that rocked my world! I knew that I was about to get a revelation on something. But what did God mean exactly? Was he talking about what was coming out of my heart and life? Or was he referring to what was coming into my home in the physical sense? I could feel the Spirit of Revelation in the room. God was getting ready to show me something and shift my thinking (Revelations belong in relationships).

"Hmmmm, what does that mean, 'What goes in must come out?'" I asked the Lord.

Silence.

He didn't answer me. I kept waiting, but I didn't hear anything. He had already done so much in our lives, but I had a feeling that God wanted me to look at another area of my life, one that he had not been invited into and had not touched before. He wanted me to take a look at the home.

My area of responsibility as wife and mother was the emotional and physical health of my family. Anyone can build a house, but it takes the heart of a mother to make a house a home. I began to see that the atmosphere inside of me would affect my home and how I ran it. For that reason, the home is a very important factor in the emotional health of my child. The adage of, "If mom is happy, then the house is happy" is so true. Autistic kids seem to be especially sensitive to picking up on that more than other kids. Not only do they emotionally pick up on things, but they process it all through their nervous and sensory systems, too. They physically feel it more. Jordan seemed to be without boundaries and was at the mercy of anything he came into contact with, feeling everything almost violently as if he was being pricked with needles or had a volt of electricity. The sound of vacuum cleaners agitated his whole body, producing fits of fear and screaming. The microwave caused him to obsessively count the numbers on the clocks and scream in shock when the timer went off. T.V attracted him to come running from wherever he was and stand like a zombie completely still and in a trance, yet partially deaf and dumb to anything else around him. Everyday things in the house affected him in ways other parents are simply not used to.

My aim was to make the home a home for him, a place to come and rest in and be healed in, so I carefully looked and watched for his reactions and behavior inside the house and came up with a long-term plan on how we could make the house a place of healing and peace. It meant that I looked at everything in and around my home: the music, food we ate, the water he bathed in or drank, chemicals in creams and soaps and cleaners, routines we had gotten used to, toys he would play with, the placement of furniture around the house, people we talked to or met with, words spoken, attitudes I thought while being around him, everything. This time I went deep into everything, and I asked God to help me reorganize my house and lifestyle completely.

Food

The first place I started was the food, his daily nutrition. As I researched more and observed him, I was really shocked at the list of Jordan's intolerances or allergies.

He could not tolerate wheat, dairy, soy, and most fruits or vegetables. Seasoning salts and MSG, different types of flour and sugar, juice and even water sources all bothered him.

We didn't go to restaurants much because we knew that if his hand touched something that had had nuts or eggs on it, then we would have to leave quickly and clean him off, administer his medication and live with the reaction for the next week or so. There were absolutely no nuts allowed in our house or anything with nuts in. Vitamins and supplements would mostly make him hyperactive because of the sugar and colorings in them or the iron that reacted with his stomach. It was exhausting to try to take care of everything on that list but also bear in mind that if we ate too much of one of the things that he wasn't allergic to, he eventually became intolerant of it later. So our list was ever-changing and growing. Soon there was hardly anything he could eat, so I one day turned out our kitchen cupboards and cleaned everything out that had any ingredients that I knew Jordan could not handle. (I had become one of those people that had to read the back of food packages for every single ingredient before I bought it and brought it home.)

For his basic menu, we had finally nailed it down to something that we trusted would not give him any kind of reaction. It was white rice, boiled chicken and carrots two to three meals every day. That was our easy menu, every day of every week. It seemed a bit boring, but it was better than the alternative of constant reactions and recovery. He didn't mind it, either. Until he was four, he had never had a French fry, or gone to a MacDonald's. Junk food, candy bars and fast food were completely out of the question. And that's how I left it.

The house

My goal in the house was to make it as allergy free, toxin free and peaceful as possible. For me to create an environment that was safe, it meant I had to do some drastic investigation work. I looked at the chemicals in creams, cleaners, beauty products, shampoos, the water supply and laundry detergents that we used in the house.

I looked at the fabrics in his room, the smells, even the trees around my house, etc. Everything that went in, around or onto his body, I researched and read up on. I cleaned as much as I could although I can't say it's my favorite thing in the world to do. I tested each thing out by removing it from the house or our routine and seeing if there was a change in his behavior. The allergies that affected him unfortunately also often played havoc with his body, causing his sensory system to overload. He would suffer for weeks on end with sleepless nights, hyperactivity, which made his stimming (repetitive movement) worse, and his mind just seemed constantly restless. If I managed to limit the allergic reactions, then I would limit the stimming and other physical autistic symptoms, too. I knew that one played off the other constantly, so I had to do something about the things that were bombarding his body.

Because of those everyday allergic reactions, he would scratch at his skin to the point that it would bleed, and I had to hold his hands down or away from doing it. I consequently adopted a drastic skin care regimen. Every two hours during the day, I would have to clean him down, with a cloth or by even bathing him and applying all his different skin creams. For most of his early life, his skin felt like sandpaper, constantly covered in scars and scabs. When his skin itched all over, he had to move all the time to make this better, as you can imagine.

Therefore, I made drastic changes in the house, and I kept it extremely clean. We washed our hands and faces, brushed our teeth and decontaminated ourselves in a manner that Haz-Mat would be proud of! The windows were kept mostly shut to reduce the outside dirt from coming in and especially the ones by his room, as the trees outside his window, he was allergic to. I made sure the house was free from clutter and dust. I cleaned the floors multiple times in the day or at least every day because in the middle of a tantrum or a stimming moment, Jordan's face would be on the floor. I cleaned his toys frequently and made sure that anything he touched in his therapy sessions was decontaminated too.

The bathrooms were always scrubbed and cleaned every day, and as he had multiple baths a day, I would always have the tub cleaned ready for the next round of cleaning up. Laundry detergents for his clothes obviously had to be hypoallergenic, as did all of our clothes because if we touched him with scratchy clothing, then that would set him off scratching for hours also.

Even the smell of strong detergents brought out hives around his face and caused his whole body to itch. He couldn't ever just take a drink from the tap when he was thirsty, as the tap water had too much chlorine in it, causing his eczema to flare up and bleed immediately. We used certain water for his drinks and something different for his bath water. The acidity level in the water made a huge difference in his behavior.

My long-term goal was for Jordan to eventually be able to lead a normal life. I wanted him to go places he wanted to go to, eat what he wanted, wear and do what he wanted, without any of the problems that we struggled with early on. His allergies were temporary, so I didn't plan for them to be in his life when he grew up. As they were temporary, I only accommodated them by setting up a skin care routine or boundaries of which they were not allowed to cross. I could never completely shield him from everything or remove them from his life completely, but I took care of everything I could.

The most important thing was that God opened up my eyes to see things for how they really were. I could see into Jordan and how he was dealing with all these things affecting him, and I could see what needed to change in the world around him. God's goal and mine was to have Jordan have a full and normal life so I planned for it.

Home

Home is a word that usually makes you feel relaxed and comfortable, a place where you look forward to being and having your family around. For me, it was the opposite. My freedom in the house seemed to decrease, and it really bothered me because I could not do a thing I needed to. I found that I could not relax and read my Bible, nor have a quiet time. My singing to the Lord in worship produced screaming fits (I am sure that I am not that bad of a singer!). I could not go to church with Jordan or worship with him in the house, I could not vacuum or clean the house because that meant the noises aggravated him and he would end up having screaming fits.

I know it sounds strange but eating became a hard thing for me to do, because I had to spend time making something for myself, which meant I had to leave him alone for a minute. I obviously could not have him with me in the kitchen because the smells or ingredients often made him break out in hives. Often, I could not eat anything that I liked because of his allergies, so I ended up skipping meals and snacks completely and only eating at strange hours or when I could get a break.

Having friends visit was impossible. Invariably, they would have touched something that made my son break out or bring something over that he could not have around him. Equally as hard were the times to go out for a walk or a park date. The environmental allergies were constant and we often had to leave and go home quickly to bathe him and administer his skin creams and allergy medicine.

I'd had enough! I decided to change some things one day. I had bent over backwards to make the house everything that my son wanted and needed. I catered everything to how he needed it, yet there still wasn't any peace or happiness in our world. I had forgotten the two other people living in the house needed it to be a home as well! So I made a wish list of everything that I wanted to have in a home. I decided that my son's needs were not going to run my house out of fear; our home needed to nourish all of us, not just an autistic child. It was more of an attitude shift from partnering with fear than about the actual changes. I could not abandon the long list of regimens I needed to fulfill every day in order to keep him free from reactions and over stimulation, but somewhere in there we needed to live, too.

With all the allergic reactions, the cleaning, the therapy, diet control and the lack of rest, there was not much about our house that made it a home. So I came up with some things that I wanted in my home that would make it home for me, too. My list was pretty simple: prayer, worship and hosting God's presence became the central core to my home environment. No fear or guilt, but freedom and love, peace and safety.

I wanted to have God's presence so tangibly with us at all times that one could feel him in our house all day and night. I wanted to be able to eat food without fear or guilt. I wanted to have people round and play dates with other children. I dreamed that my home would nurture and bring up godly children, that the norm inside would be one of miracles and healings. So I made the dream list and planned on it all coming to pass one day. I made slow changes that eventually made the house a home, and it became a place where Jordan could actually relax and enjoy himself and where I could do what I needed to relax, too.

Praying over him

During the day, I would pray over Jordan and lay my hands on him, whenever I thought of something else that he needed to be released into him. I learned that nothing happens in the kingdom without first a declaration, so I began to call forth, in faith, who my son was created to be. I constantly found more and more things to declare over him and call him. I called him "peaceful one" and "blessed little man of God."

Some of the things that I did were not easy at first. He did not like me praying over him at first because I would make him sit still! And if there was one thing he hated, it was to be sitting still. I didn't want him to see prayer as a torture device!! I also tried to get him to look at me in the eyes while I declared things over him, which he also did not like. He got used to me saying things like, "You are incredible, you are amazing, you can do all things through Christ who strengthens you," and he eventually after months and years, sat still and listened when I blessed him. The more he could handle it, the more I took the opportunity to release word blessings over him. I wanted him to know God's presence and be at peace when he was being prayed for. I wanted him to know he could trust me and trust that my words were going to be good for him. I needed him to understand God's heart, which was to bless him and see him prosper. So I took those times to declare things from the word of God over him and release promises. Sometimes I sang to him while I did his therapy and massages.

Scriptures that I prayed and declared include:

Isaiah 61

Psalm 139

1 Timothy 1:7

The Blood of Jesus Christ

I know without any doubt that there is nothing that the blood of Jesus cannot take care of. There is no sickness or viral strain or bacteria so advanced that won't be bowled over by the blood of Jesus. I know that His blood can take care of it all. Jesus didn't skimp on the cross; he gave it his all, so why should we skimp in using the full power of what Jesus paid for in our everyday lives? Jordan and I would take communion together every day. Communion is a meal that heals. It's not only the elements of the bread and wine, but also the implications of the cross and our lives in Christ Jesus that brings healing. Communion is also the renewing of a love covenant with God. It's like saying "I do" every day to your beloved and renewing your vows of devotion to God. So I put that into our everyday routine. Every night before bed, Jordan and I would take it together and pray. I explained it to him, and every night he would fall asleep right afterwards.

Music

Like most other autistic kids, his hearing was extremely sensitive, and noises physically hurt a lot. Noises like the vacuum cleaner or blender made him scream and shake his head side to side or have screaming fits on the floor. The funny thing was that music on the TV was fine for him. The moment I turned off the TV and put on a CD of worship music instead, well that would set him off screaming. It had been my dream to have a house that was filled with worship music 24/7, so I had to find a way to incorporate what my dream was slowly into the day and get him used to praise and worship music. I did what I could. I played it quietly in the background, or put it on my headphones. I had to worship God and sing.

There was no question about that. It sustained me and focused my heart towards heaven. Jordan having screaming fits during worship times or my quiet times was not helpful, to say the least. He would run over to the CD player banging his head and scream at it or at me for singing and raising my hands to God. But I am a worshiper; I have never been able to shut myself up from singing and I didn't want autism to shut me up, either. I could not take care of my son the way he needed if I did not get time with God.

You cannot merely survive in a relationship with God; it's his dream to have you thrive. And I needed to thrive, no matter what else was going on in my life or around me. I could not bring heaven to earth without being in God's presence and worshiping him first. I felt like I was to create a tabernacle of David, where worship and prayer were constantly lifted up. God doesn't stay away from a home like that! So I tried to make music in general fun instead of aggravating to his senses. I only played Christian artists who had a God focus to their songs because I knew their heart behind the music. Jordan eventually got used to hearing worship music playing in our house most of the day. He began to like soaking music and classical music as well as I played them during the therapy I would do with him or the massages I would give him.

I made up cute songs to sing to him in a funny voice, telling him how amazing he was. When he was young and couldn't speak properly, I would just sing over him and he would laugh away at me. When he got older, he started to reply to my wacky tunes. I would sing, "You're so awesome." He would say, "Yes, I am so awesome." I would sing next, "You are so precious." He would reply, "Yes, I am so precious." I would follow with, "You are so clever." He would say, "Yes, I am so clever." We had fun being spontaneous and making up funny songs to lift his spirit. Eventually, after years of my singing over him and not giving up on drumming into him just how amazing he is, he got it. I tried to make music part of his therapy; sometimes music can enter parts of a human's heart and life that the average everyday cannot.

Soaking times

I didn't really know what soaking was until I realized that I had spent most of my life doing that very thing! Growing up, I would put on a worship CD, lie down and sing in tongues for hours. When I got older and had a house and family to take care of, my soaking lifestyle changed. When Jordan was older and we had moved into our own house, I took one room and made it into a prayer room with worship music playing constantly.

I found that soaking music released a peace into my whole house day and night. Once I had gotten used to soaking and worshiping him in that place, it transformed my prayer times. Soaking is purely focusing on God, and I didn't want to bring my troubles into a soaking time to the point where I couldn't worship him. I feel like I left my troubles at the door of the throne room and got lost in his presence. I learned to soak first, praise him, and worship him.

Soaking is for kids as well, and I don't think you could not expect them to be like an adult and take every opportunity to sit down and focus on him quietly, not moving! Kids think about God's presence differently than we often do. God doesn't desire or accept only adult relationships. He made himself available to all ages, all minds, and to people in all walks of life. But on top of having relationships 24/7 with all ages, he enjoys all those ages, too. Otherwise, you would encounter a side of Father God's character with a hole in it. He doesn't bypass or ignore children and wait until they are older so he can talk properly to them. So while we try to make the kids act like an adult in a relationship with God, he on the other hand, never asks them to be anything other then who they are right then with him. I know that he loves the way kids interact with him. He looks forward to being with them, so we have to find a way to invite God to interact with our kids with Holy Spirit and soaking times. It is also a fact that soaking is different for every person. Whether your children play quietly on the floor beside you or spin or dance with flags, get their drums out and make some music, it's up to them and God. Maybe they will want to draw or read books while you lie down and quiet your spirit or they may want to play dress up with Jesus and make up a play.

Whatever it is, soaking in his presence cultivates life. I had Jordan close his eyes beside me as I played some soaking music, and he would often have encounters and visions when he did. It did not happen over night and took him some time to get used to being able to handle the music throughout his body. Also, he had to try to control his hyperactivity while he was lying on the floor. Sometimes he wanted to paint his visions out, and sometimes he just played, but I tried to get him used to the presence and sensitive to Holy Spirit.

Bedtime

Jordan's bedtime routine became my masterpiece! It is the thing I worked on more than anything else because I treasured my sleep as most parents do. With all the trouble we had establishing sleep patterns and the complete lack of naps, I set up "THE routine."

I watched and protected my son during the day, spoke words of life over him, prayed for him, watched what he ate, guarded the atmosphere around him and made home a place of healing. I thought I should take as much care with his nighttime, too. Just because the lights went out it, didn't mean that the prayers or protection should cease. There is a mystery about sleep and what happens when we rest; it's supernatural, and I don't think that it is fully understood. I made it a point to make bedtime so drenched in love and protection that when I left the room, he could sleep in peace. I wanted to teach him how to rest properly, something that I think a lot of autistic spectrum children don't know how to do well.

So I got Jordan used to winding down slowly, and I read to him quietly. I held him and prayed over him in tongues or sang in tongues. I made a point to invite heaven and the Father in at night to take over the night watch. Psalm 121:3 says, "He who watches over you shall never sleep nor slumber." God likes rest; he promotes it for our good and fit it into creation. He desires us to rest properly, so we have to find a way to cultivate and honor that rest.

Therefore, I wanted a routine that taught Jordan who he was, a routine that brought him close to God and invited heaven to be near. I wanted him to know that nighttime meant sleep and rest. I spent time praying over him at night and made sure he was comfortable with me praying for long periods over him. He needed to be comfortable with the presence of God, so I asked for God's presence to be all over the house, and especially, in his room. While he was busy elsewhere in the house, I would go into his room and pray before he went to sleep in it. I spoke to his pillow and declared that when he lay his head on it, that he would find rest and healing and growth. I took his sheets and blanket and prayed that Holy Spirit would dwell in them and cover him with comfort and protection, etc. I worshiped and read my Bible in his room and paced up and down on the rug, declaring promises of God over the walls and furniture.

The other thing I worked hard on was his bath time before bed. I had to spend and still do spend a lot of time taking care of his skin after the bath. The nighttime is the best time for skin to heal and rest, so I took the opportunity to speak to his skin as I massaged the medical creams in, telling the eczema to go and for healthy skin to grow back. We then would read a lot of Bible stories before I settled him in bed, too, and had gotten him into the routine of only thinking about the word of God, his promises and his presence before he slept. Then it was prayer time. The first thing I taught him to memorize was the Lord's Prayer; then he would pray for the peace of Jerusalem and then for Israel. He would pray for the orphans and needy people around the world, and lastly I taught him to declare nighttime blessings over himself. As he grew, I also taught him Hebrew nighttime prayers and blessings, and he would also pray those before he slept. He got accustomed to the routine like he had seen me doing it. After he had done all that, we took communion together.

I made a big deal out of his routine and didn't rush through it. Sometimes I would take up to two hours or more just to get him bathed, covered with all the right creams, read to, prayed over, etc. I put things in his routine that taught him how to rest, who he was in Christ, how to take care of his body and mind before bed and habits that would carry into the rest of his life. Again, I had in mind that one day he would be healed and would have this routine in his life that taught him to rest properly. Or that one day when he was a father, himself, that he would teach his children the same things.

Blessings

One of the cultures I love because of their ability to speak blessings and have the importance and high regard for words is the Jewish culture. I started learning some basic Hebrew a few years ago. I was fascinated with the language and loved studying it, especially the blessings and prayers. There is something so precious about praying in other languages. I thought that it would be a good therapy tool to teach him to use his mouth and brain for blessing and to learn other languages. He learned them really quickly. I had them printed out and added into his speech therapy that I incorporated into our daily routine. He was amazing and could say them by heart after a week. I wanted to get him used to using his mouth for blessing himself and others, instead of using the classic autistic incoherent phrases or lines from T.V shows that made no sense. I tried to teach him that his mouth has the power to create things in his life and the world around him. I taught him what comes out of his mouth is either gold or garbage. He gets to choose which one it will be because out of the heart the mouth speaks. If good words go in, good words come out.

Honestly, it took me a few years to get used to blessings. I had not grown up thinking that words were that important and didn't hold them in high regard. I did not use my mouth to bless as much as I should have. I became more careful about the words I said around him and the words I said to him.
I took the opportunity to bless him with the opposite of what he was acting like. If he was having trouble with playing, I would sing and bless him with words that contradicted what I saw. If he was flapping his arms when he was excited, I blessed his peace and love for people. I would read the Bible to him while he lay in my lap and get him used to hearing the Word of God. I read the Bible stories that inspired us. I have a few that I felt God had assigned to him as his mission statement for his healing and for his life, one of which is Isaiah 61 (Jordan knows it by heart). His Bible was and is always by his bed. I taught him to read it during the day and before bed, so he could have the Word of God and the stories in his memory during the day and the last thing before he fell asleep at night.

Intercession

I asked God to transform my intercession from whining and crying out in desperation to power, activated by faith. I was tired of shooting in the dark with my prayers and not seeing anything change. I had to get close enough to God to see things from his perspective. Bill Johnson says that persistence in prayer doesn't change God; it shapes us for the answer. I didn't understand that until a lot further down the road in my prayer life.

God never asked me to stop hurting because of what we were going through, but He did want to help. He wanted to partner with us in transformation. I learned I should not pray from that painful place of defeat or anger or abandonment. I had to pray *with* God, partner with him, share his view and perspective and pray from victory.

In prayer, I needed to have an exchange of vision and perspective, a change in focus from defeat to one of clear victory. When I walked into my prayer closet and walked out with my burdens still attached, then I just whined to God. I learned to walk in with a mind of humanity and walk out with a mindset of Christ. With the mind of Christ, of faith, and of heaven, my prayers became different, and my world could not help but change.

The exchange of mindsets took place when I gave up my rights to try to drag God down to my level of vision to get him to see only what I saw. In reality, I needed to go up to his penthouse level suite and see a situation from where he is. One level is temporal and earthly, while the other is based in eternity and heaven. When something overwhelmed me and I could not see or I didn't know how to pray, I went to God for a better view. When I aligned myself with his view of a situation, I prayed differently. I knew God's character to be loving and consistently good and that he uses me and my life to change the world around me. I would not repeat what is seemingly impossible down here and remind him of the obstacles that I face. A tapestry is always a mess of threads and colors from underneath. From up top, I bet it looked beautiful.

So, that was a list of all the things that I included and changed in our home. I did what I felt I should do. It was a lot of work, but I wanted to be purposeful and intentional with the life that God had left for me to use and take care of the one that he had asked me to (Jordan).

Chapter 10

The Prayers

It's probably one of the biggest and most important questions I get asked. What did I do? How did I pray? Bit by bit God dealt with me, healed me, helped me change our lives and house around. We got Jordan therapy and prayed over him constantly, changed his diet and put together a routine of things that invited God into his life. It was a lot of work and well worth it. But the prayers came out of my walk with God, and it's from your walk with God that your breakthrough will come.

Go to God for your own insight. Get your ideas and revelations personally from the Father. But start your own journey with God into his heart, and do not underestimate the importance of the power of your walk with God. Remember who you are and what his death on the cross gave you. The enemy would love to keep you at a place where you believe that you're not worthy or you are a failure, you are not important and can't have a miracle. That's a lie, and the only thing you can bet on with the enemy is that he will ALWAYS lie to you. You have a mandate to be a life-changer, breakthrough facilitator, and prayer warrior down here. You are called to bring heaven to earth.

I encourage you to mix the highest quality of faith into your prayers. Don't skimp on it. Faith attracts God's attention. Having faith is like building a landing strip for God's supply plane to land on. The wider the landing strip, the larger the plane that is able to land on it. Faith is like pouring tarmac on the runway and turning on the lights so the plane can see where it has to land. God can't help but respond with his jet plane packed with supplies for the land of your life.

Pray for your children, that they will have all that God wants to give them in their lives. They are tomorrow's leaders, and our ceiling is their floor. What we build for them to stand on today will build a nation and our world tomorrow. Release the promise over them that they have a future and a hope. Speak words of life over them so they know who they are. Children who know who they are and who their Father is, act completely different than orphans do. Release the kingdom of heaven in your home and in your parenting, fasting and praying for your children.

Ask Jesus to help you bring life to your child and ask to have his view of the whole situation. If you only see what is ahead of you and what the enemy is doing, but fail to see what God sees, then your vision is not quite where it should be. See what God says about your situation, and do a swap for his long-term goal for their life. See what his answer is for your struggle, and pray that in. Having heaven's perspective of a situation is the key to changing lives.

My prayers before He healed my mind went something like this, "Oh, God, why did you do this? Why me? Where are you and why aren't you helping me with this? Come down and do something. This isn't fair. What did I do to deserve this? Ahhh. Where are you, God? This is too hard for me.... Amen." (As if that attitude has ever got anyone anywhere!) My prayers had no faith in them, and I sounded like a whining child who wasn't getting her way. I was angry and desperate and not getting anywhere. That in fact wasn't prayer; it was airing a bad attitude that needed to die!

My prayers after he renewed my mind went something like this: "Dear Father, help me pray because I don't know what I am supposed to say to you. Help me understand what I am supposed to do about this hard situation. I need you and I can't do this alone. Amen." At least here I was surrendered and ready to listen to him in case he answered me. Here is where I just had abandoned the stinky attitude and had gotten on my knees ready for the signpost to pop up to point the way to breakthrough.

And once I had gotten who I was finally into my mind and could see Father God properly, I knew what I could pray for and what I was supposed to declare. In the last part of my prayer journey I got to a place where I used strong declarative prayers.

So in this part I wanted to share with you the prayers I prayed and the visions I prayed through when God shared them with me. God had changed my identity and my prayer life, but I was lacking focus on what to go after in specific prayer for Jordan. I felt I had gotten down his routine and taken care of the everyday life things that he needed. Now I needed a vision to inspire my prayers. It was kind of like being a sniffer dog and needing a target to go after. At that stage, my first prayers were filled with hunger for revelation.

Here is one of the first prayers I prayed:

Heavenly Father, I come to you today to ask for help. I ask that you will give me your plans, your prayers, your declarations for my child. I ask heavenly Father for you to give me your view, your solutions, your words and your heart for my child. Give me your strength and your grace, your mercy and your patience for my son. Sustain my vision for this healing. Keep my eyes sharp and on course. Shut off my ears to the negative and damaging words that would not bring life, but open my ears to the Holy Spirit so I can hear the beautiful sound of his voice. Start me on my course, stir my heart as yours is stirred and give me insight directly from your view on your throne. Help me, Father. Help me to see, speak and release all that is from your heart today. And thank you. Thank you for your Holy Spirit and for what you did on the cross. Thank you, Jesus. I love you and need you. Come be with me today. Amen.

Here is another one:

Father, I want to pray your prayers for my child. I want to know what you want for my child. I want to know what you say about him and what I am to say about him. I want to know your heart for him so I can release those words over him and see the breakthrough that I know is in your heart today for him. Let my words not be empty, but full of your light and life and love. I desire to connect to you and hear you. I desire to know you more. Father, I want to know you and know Your heart, and I want these prayers to come out of that relationship. I want to stay close to you and depend upon every word that comes out of your mouth. Father, I need you and I cannot do this alone. I ask for you to come and draw me closer to your side. I ask to partner with you and I ask for the authority to release heaven upon earth and all your dominion on earth and in our lives here. Amen

I started with those prayers because I had nowhere else to start from. The prayers were really simple, but simplicity is the best place to be with God. My heart desire was for an exchange to take place, where I would swap my limited knowledge and vision for his vision of this whole thing. I had a feeling that I was about to walk through a door and into a room where the secrets were held. But before I could get the secrets or understand them, I had to spend a long time on my face just waiting for a breakthrough, hungry for his voice and his word to be released.

2 Chronicles 7:14 (NLT) Then if my people who are called by my name will humble themselves and pray and seek my face and turn from their wicked ways, I will hear from heaven and will forgive their sins and restore their land.

Chapter 11

Vision #1

So I say to you: Ask and it will be given to you; seek and you will find; knock and the door will be opened to you. For everyone who asks receives; the one who seeks finds; and to the one who knocks, the door will be opened.

Luke 11:9 – 11

Again it started with a desperate prayer:

Lord I believe you have set apart my son for great things and you have called him by name, and he is yours. Please show me what needs to happen in my son's life and in his healing. Let me help release Your healing into his life, and please help me understand what I am to do. Amen."

I remember as I prayed that, right before my eyes again flashed a scene of a badly built house. It was tilting to one side, like the leaning Tower of Pisa and was falling apart, badly. It seemed there was a cracked foundation supporting this rickety old house. Sitting on top of this house was a poor excuse for a roof, with roof tiles on the ground around it and gaping holes exposing the insides. The windows were all shattered, and the front door was flapping in the wind back and forth hanging by one small screw on the hinge. The siding was all falling off, and whenever a wind blew, more pieces fell off the already worse for wear excuse for a house. The sky was grey and rainy, domineering clouds filled the sky, and the wind was blowing mercilessly around.

The land on which this house stood seemed dark and run down, water logged by the bad drainage and holes in the ground while bits of the house lay sprawled across the grass. I did not like the look of this house and I knew God was showing me it was my son's life or his mind.

This vision immediately reminded me of where God started with me: the same kind of land, the same weather and the same looking house. I felt like I had a job to do, to partner with Jesus and combine my words and prayers with his to see change and breakthrough for my son. Just as Jesus did with my house by taking it down piece by piece, I needed to partner with God on this project and walk slowly and carefully. So I started praying.

I used each part of the house for symbolism. For example, the siding could be the protection that he would have set up or the barriers covering the structure of his life. The windows could be the places that he watches the world from, a point of exposure yet distant from the outside world. I treated the inside of the house as if it were the inside of his mind or soul. I treated the land the house was built on as if it were the foundations given to him from generations past.

First, I focused my prayers on taking the siding off. Then I saw the interior walls and then the exterior walls, the roof, the doors, the window frames come off. Bit by bit, each little piece came down and was thrown onto a pile off to the side. That left the foundation. As I looked closely at it, I could see the cracks and see how slanted it was. What are you supposed to do with a broken, slanted foundation? Break it up as Jesus had done with mine. I saw a hammer come down and start banging away at it, breaking it up. I thought, "Wow, God, that's hard." But he said, "There is no other way to break up a foundation than to literally break it up with a hammer." I watched as God broke it up, leaving a pile of stones and concrete. In my vision, out of the sky, I saw this awesome shining new foundational slab being laid. It looked like a merger of many different gemstones, shining like a rainbow in the sun. It was almost see through, yet almost pure gold. It looked so beautiful. The old was gone, and the new had been laid.

Prayer for the broken house

Father, I ask for you to come now. I invite you to show me how you want to start this process in my child's life. Show me what you want me to do, show me how to partner with you on this and not hinder you during this period. I ask for you to dismantle the house that has stood as the structure in my son's life until now. Take down the old ways of thinking, take down the broken shelter and build him up to be the person you want him to be. I welcome you in now to start the work in my child's life. I welcome your processes, your timing, your wisdom, your hand and most importantly, your love, Father. I ask for grace over me during this period so that I can walk in peace and truth. Tear up what is not working, take away what is not supposed to be there, remove all burdens and curses, in Jesus' name. Holy Spirit, I ask for you to be our constant Guide, Comforter and Voice during this time. I ask for grace to flow like oil over both our lives and for protection as we start this process together. I ask that you will help us not to pick up the old and put it into the new house. I pray what you dismantle and throw away, will stay away forever. I praise you for who you are. I thank you for what you are doing and what you are about to do and for the life of my child. I pray this, in Jesus' name, now. Amen.

Generational curses

To hear "Oh, its just bad genes," or "It's just a quirky family trait," made me want to yell! I didn't want to inherit the bad, the weak, or cursed ways of thinking, and I didn't want it for my son, either. I didn't want to look forward to Daddy's thinning hairline or Mom's mood swings! I wanted to be free, and I didn't want to accept a family trait or weakness in my line or blame it for acting out bad behaviors and sinning. I wanted to get rid of the things that were not in God's heart for me.

While I know that some people don't even believe that things can be passed from generation to generation and might pass it off as just a bad family trait, still deep down they don't want to keep it in their lives.

Why would we keep it in the family when we have the option to remove it? We are supposed to be going from glory to glory. If that's the case, then things that hold us back or tie us down are not supposed to come along for the ride in our lives. I would rather get rid of the junk in my trunk and leave that space for the goodness of God to fill in.

If you want old Grandpa John's bad heart conditions, or your father's receding hair to come and pay a visit, then go ahead and leave it where it is lodged. Neurology research shows that you can turn on and off your genes[1]. It gives you something to think about, doesn't it? But for me personally, I would rather activate the DNA of God in me and leave the bad stuff in the grave where it belongs. I just want what God has promised us. Simple. God said we are a new creation in Christ, the old has gone and the new has come, so what does that practically look like walked out in our lives today?

I felt a great joy about this part of my journey. The thought of getting rid of curses from my DNA or traits that I didn't want was great for me. More importantly, I wanted it to be out of my son's life and have him free. While I know I personally did nothing to make some of these things happen, like sin or curses that affected generations before me, I was now taking a place of asking for forgiveness and interceding for a breakthrough for them. When I took the joy of intercession in hand and stood in the place of those people that had sinned, I had the opportunity to bring heaven to earth and remove what was holding us back. Having the opportunity to repent is an amazing privilege. Seeing it from God's perspective is joyful, too. I can go into the place of repenting with a thankful heart and have the blood of Jesus remove everything that is not supposed to be in my life and my child's. Jesus made a way with his blood. His death on the cross made a way for us to be set free from every sin and disease. While I repented for my forefathers, I also had to repent for my personal sins that could be running in the veins of my child. Never underestimate the power of the prayer of repentance. Jesus took our place on the cross and took all the curses and sins ever committed, so that we could have life.

I got books on inner healing and read the Hunters' books on physical healing. I listened to Arthur Burke's series on blessing your spirit and read books by Robert Mcgee, including, The Search for Significance.

I read through Dr Caroline Leaf's book called <u>Who Switched Off My Brain?</u> Which helped when I needed to change my thinking and gave me hope to change the thought processes that I was stuck in. There are lots of resources on this subject that can bless your life and open up the way to healing. But it is important to pray and see where the Lord wants you to start. There is so much information out there that God will show you to do and what book to read and what prayer to pray. If you lack insight or wisdom, ask for it. He will never refuse a request for more wisdom or understanding.

I sat down one day after I had read some of the books listed above and started to ask God where I should start or how I should start to pray. I knew what I wanted to say. But it was a really important prayer for me to say out loud to him, so I sat down and wrote out what I wanted to say. Here is what I prayed:

I come before you, Father, and confess the sins that I myself, my father and mother, as well as my forefathers have committed. I ask for your forgiveness and ask for you to cleanse my blood line, my DNA, my character and body, of all debts incurred by my forefathers that are being carried over into my life and my son's life. Lord, I don't know exactly what they are and cannot call them all out by name, but I come on their behalf and stand before you to say sorry. I confess the sins of my fathers and ask for forgiveness and I ask that the blood of Jesus will wipe away all the sins. I ask, God, for you to remove all the curses and the consequences of those sins and curses from my life now and from the life of my son. You died to set us free and to pay the price, so I ask for your blood to take care of it all, now. Cleanse my family line, all the way back to Adam, and remove all curses from us, today. Bless us, Lord, make us fruitful and whole. I ask for your grace now. I ask for mercy to cover us and to fill us with your love, now. You are God of all. You are Lord of my life. I serve you alone and love you. My life is yours, and so is my son's. I pray for life to be restored where it was taken due to sin and curses. Amen.

I prayed this prayer for my son:

Lord, I want to thank you for my child. Thank you for lending him to me. I lift his life, his spirit, his body and his mind up to you, now. I ask, God, for the insight into his life and for the things that could have been passed on to him from generations past.

In the name of Jesus, I cut off all curses that are generational all the way back to Adam to this present day. I break them off, in the name of Jesus, and speak life over him, in Jesus' name. Any pledges and promises made by my forefathers to any other gods, people, or groups, I denounce them and break them off him, in Jesus' name. All witchcraft, all idolatry, and all rebellion against Father God, I denounce and reject it for him, in Jesus' name. Please forgive us for our sins that we have committed against you. I ask for the blood of Jesus Christ to cleanse him and may the blood go all the way back to Adam removing any threads of curses, sins and word curses from my and his generational line.

I pray for complete release from the things that could hinder my son being restored as a child of God and living in completeness of that. I call my son a child of God, adopted into the family of God and with that, I pray that all the blessings that come from being adopted as a child will be his. I pray that all the blessings of Abraham will be his. All the things that you promised, I pray into his life. I pray for life to come into him where there has been death. Again, I pray for life to come where the lands of his life were once dedicated to something other than you, God. I pray for the wholeness of shalom from heaven to be upon his mind. I dedicate my son to you for all the days of his life to serve you and love you. Amen.

Rejection and isolation between brain parts

Rejection often passes in generational lines. Rejection from parents or teachers, friends or siblings can set a life pattern in motion. The effects of rejection cut deep into a person's mind and spirit.

Often, if there has been an orphan spirit already affecting them, then rejection will inflame an already painful wound making survival tactics take over their thinking (fear of man, attention seeking, rejecting others, offended spirit, un-forgiveness).

The breakthrough will come when they have a love encounter with the Father and hope is released. Rejection is also one of the things that brings isolation into a person's life and I believe that it quickly goes deep into the brain, reformatting the way we think.
When we harbor offense, it cuts off vital connections that we make to other humans, and I believe that it also does something deep in our thinking. We need one another and have to remember that the devil came to steal, kill and destroy so anything that looks like his handiwork needs to be kicked out.

The way rejection works is almost in secret, started by a lie with the sole purpose of cutting off one from another, whether it is a person in your family or church. One part says it's too different to be accepted by the other and a split occurs (Remember one of Satan's names is "splitter"). The moment you see anything that would split one from the other then a lie is present, creating a wedge. When lies enter into your thinking or mind, you align yourself with it and take on it's characteristics, making a copy of the problem to multiply over and over again. So that's in the life outside the body, but what about inside the brain. I felt like there were areas that were separated from one another in Jordan's brain, for example mirror neurons were not activated or were too few in number and could not connect to other areas of the brain.

I prayed for all areas of his little brain to be connected once again in case emotional, physical and psychological injuries had disconnected them. I also felt like speech and memory centers were not communicating properly to each other, preventing memory recall, etc., to function properly. I wanted a harmony from heaven where all the centers of the brain would be realigned connected, alive and functioning as God intended.

Here is a prayer I prayed to do with rejection in the brain:

Father, I speak to this brain of my child, and I ask that you will release a sound of love and acceptance over him today.

I pray that your love will wipe away every tear and deep wound of rejection. I pray that you will forgive us if we have hurt him as his parents or if any other person has hurt him. I say that this whole person is wanted, and accepted and has a purpose and an assignment in God. God, your love is the only answer to our problems, and your love is the only answer my son needs.

Wipe every tear from his eyes that are caused by rejection and coat him with grace like oil so that no offense sticks to him.

Father, in the name of Jesus, I ask that you will heal any wounds inflicted on him by rejection that are promoting isolation now. Lord, will you come in your fullness and open up his heart again? Will you reconnect his mind and his soul and his being together and remove from him all the distractions and wedges that don't allow connection.

Father, I pray that he will grasp just how much he is loved and wanted. I pray that your love will chase him down all the days of his life and will constantly catch him. God, invade his life with your love, bowl him over, overload his heart and life with the greatest love that he has ever known. Let the physical revelation of the healing come to his mind now and set his mind free from lies that hinder how you desire for his mind to function. I speak truth over his mind, love over the neurons and connections, love over every pathway and freedom to be himself. I pray a core of love will resound deep in his heart and so demolishing all lies that come against who you say you are and how much he is loved by you Father... Amen.

I prayed this blessing over him, too, at night and during the day when I laid hands on him:

I bless you, in the name of Jesus, and I say no matter who does or doesn't want you in this life, GOD does. He planned for you before you even existed. I say that you are wanted and loved and planned for. I speak to your spirit, and I say that you existed in God's heart before the foundations of the earth were laid and you will be with God for all eternity. I speak shalom over your brain, over your life and over your spirit now. I bless you, in the name of Jesus.

Bible verses:

Jeremiah 1:5

Before I formed you in the womb I knew you, before you were born I set you apart; I appointed you as a prophet to the nations.

Psalm 139:13-18

For you created my inmost being; you knit me together in my mother's womb. I praise you because I am fearfully and wonderfully made; your works are wonderful, I know that full well. My frame was not hidden from you when I was made in the secret place, when I was woven together in the depths of the earth. Your eyes saw my unformed body; all the days ordained for me were written in your book before one of them came to be. How precious to me are your thoughts, God! How vast is the sum of them! Were I to count them, they would outnumber the grains of sand—when I awake, I am still with you.

1 Timothy 2:7

For God hath not given us the spirit of fear; but of power, and of love, and of a sound mind.

<u>Toxins in the brain</u>

Lord, I pray against toxins; metals; viruses; bacteria lingering in, affecting, or deteriorating my child's brain. Lord you can dissolve metal and anything that comes again the truth of your word that says no weapon formed against him will prosper. In Jesus name I command all foreign substances to leave his physical brain now and to never hinder my son again. Loose yourself and leave in the name of Jesus.
 Anything wrapped around his neurons, anything wrapped around DNA or stuck in the blood vessels, LEAVE now in Jesus name. Loose his mind, you are trespassing and you have outstayed your welcome.

Lord, I also ask that you will make any weak places in my son's brain where things can easily affect him to now become strong and protected, in Jesus' name. If there has been any damage, I speak the opposite over it, and release life over the affected area in Jesus' name, right now.

*I plead the blood of Jesus over every part of his mind and say to them that if there is any lack of growth and healing in heaven for healthy minds so there will be no lack in your life son. Nothing will take ahold of my child's brain; nothing will hold it captive or cause anything other than life to take shape there. I say my sons mind is a breeding ground for breakthrough, for heaven to descend upon it, for wholeness and peace and it will multiply throughout his entire being. I pray freedom to the brain and all it's pathways. I super impose over him now the intentions, the truth, the decree and the Shalom of heaven for his mind in Jesus name. I declare: **you win, my child because Jesus already won**. Amen.*

Who switched off my brain?: controlling toxic thoughts and emotions
Caroline Leaf - Inprov, Ltd. – 2009

Chapter 12

Vision #2

I spent nearly a year praying what God had shown me in the previous vision and over my son. It was sometimes hard to keep praying because I didn't see any major significant changes, but I knew what I was praying into his life were seeds and that someday I would see them sprout somewhere. I was doing everything I knew I could and speaking life over him as much as I could. I prayed all those prayers over him with the vision always in the back of my mind of being rebuilt by Jesus' hand. I was soaking him in prayer and words of life, no matter what I daily saw in front of me. God's promises and realities always override what we see in front of us. And no matter how hard it gets, from his reality, we pray. So I repeated my prayers and declarations over him day in and day out, sometimes praying the same thing again and again for months until I felt released to go on to something else to pray for.

One day I was so exhausted by the homeschooling, therapy and praying constantly that I cried out to God. I had been praying for so long for Jordan to be healed and for him to grow and change. I knew there had to be more! I raised my voice and said:

*Father, you need to do more than you are doing. You said you would help me. I am feeling like I am not getting anywhere and it's been years of praying and not seeing any major results. Enough God. You need to help me like never before. Give me a clear vision and show me what is going on inside his mind now, so I can know what to pray for please. **Please**. I need your help. Amen.*

Immediately God showed me another vision. At first, I heard the wind howling and blowing. Then the picture of a highway came into view. It was poorly lit up because the lampposts were all blown out. The sky was black, filled with dark overpowering clouds as if a storm had been raging in the area. The wind was rushing through the trees, and everything looked like it had been shaken by an earthquake or a tornado. There was a long, gray road that went to an island from either another island or from the mainland. But the road had been torn up and badly damaged, the surface was cracked and chunks of it were missing. The lines on the road were stripped of paint. No car could drive on that kind of a road. It badly needed repairing. The bridge leading to this island had no lights or lampposts, the railings were missing and the foundations seemed to have been shaken. I knew the scene represented my son's brain and that the roads were his neural pathways. It was time to go after some neurological things and release God's presence over his brain now.

God was giving me insight for how to pray for him. This time I heard God say to me: *"Look at the road, the land Liz. What would you like to see happen to that island and to this road? What you want to see is what you speak out. Start repairing it with your prayers."* Immediately, I started praying for the lights to go up all along the road. I called for power to go on again and to connect to the main land and light up the pathways. I saw the lights come in and the vision change before my very eyes. The section of road was lit and I could now see the extent of the damage on the road.

As I looked at the broken road, I started calling things out as if I was the only repair crew that came along to clean up. I commanded the surface to become safe, smooth and drivable again. I told the rocks and lumps of stone to get off and out of the way. I prayed for the foundations of the road to be strong. Once again, I saw the vision change and what looked like a mess before was becoming a freshly paved road. As I carried on praying through what I wanted to see, one by one I could see each section of this vision change until I saw what looked like a normal road. Then I started to pray for signposts to direct traffic along and to this place. As this was a representation of his mind, I knew to have a healthy fully functioning mind you needed every part of the brain communicating with each other. This road needed to be repaired so that it could be connected to other parts of the land. Sure enough, minutes later I saw big green highway signs come up.

After I saw that vision I knew that I was to move onto praying over this now instead of the previous one. I focused on how I would rebuild the road and the connections, I chose words that went along with what I wanted to see and with my prayers I touched upon what heaven wanted to release over my sons mind. For months I carried on praying those prayers. I kept going back to the vision I had seen and laid hands on my son's head to speak the very same things over him. I spent months sometimes just praying over one area such as the flooded island or the network of roads going through or around the island. I didn't feel a release until I saw the vision change and saw some changes in my son.

Chapter 13

More prayers

The vision I saw represented Jordan's mind and the state of where his mind was at. It clearly showed me what I had to do and how I was supposed to pray. God had lovingly asked me to create the things he needed in his mind with my prayers. The destruction of the land by natural disasters like storms, hurricanes and floods had resulted in debris blocking communication to other parts of his mind, impassable roads and fields of the harvest ruined. I saw that I needed to use the power of God's Holy Spirit in my prayers to clear, repair and rebuild him from the inside out.

Prayer:

Lord, a storm has raged inside my child's mind and has caused destruction where there should have been a thriving life. Father, I lift my child up to you and ask that you will restore to him all that was broken, all that was lost, all that was destroyed and all that was carried away. I pray that my son's mind will come to be at rest. I pray that where flooding has occurred, a flood of sensations, frequencies or emotions and feelings, that you will now provide him boundaries
I speak boundaries to the sea, boundaries to the weather and land, roads, etc. I ask for your Spirit to dry up the water within his mind that has overwhelmed him. Clear his mind, and make it new. Make it bright, make it strong and make it pleasing to you. I pray for the sun to come out in the land of his mind and bring your life, your love, your warmth, your comfort, your peace and your growth. Clear away the debris and remove all blockages that were left and are not allowing the land to be alive.

Take away the things that hold him back from thinking as you intended him to think.

Restore all the different parts of his brain, Father from which freedom and life have been taken away, and I ask for supernatural restoration for his life, his mind. I speak total restoration over him. Not half or partial, but complete restoration in Jesus' name. Lord, you said ask and you shall receive, so right now, I ask for total restoration for this beautiful mind. Jesus, you died so that we can have life and life to the full. You have redeemed us with your blood. You redeemed us. You died, and you said, "It is finished." I want the full life that you intended for my son, now. I ask for everything that you died to give us back, to be restored. Restore his mind to think like you made it to think. Restore his mind to act and coordinate like you made it to. Restore to him the blueprints from which we were created. Restore the ancient pathways, the pathways which they had before the fall. You said that we can have the mind of Christ so I ask for that now.

I speak to his mind now and say that the winter has passed, the storms have gone down and the sun has come out now. It is time. Wake up in Jesus' name. I speak that this season is a time of growth. No more deadness of winter, no more mere survival. I speak life. Son, your mind will be a well efficient, working, complimentary, peaceful and well established working tool. Redeem and restore him, Lord. Amen.

Flooding of the land

I felt like Jordan's brain was being overloaded and the pathways couldn't handle the sounds, environmental and nerve/sensory input that it was being bombarded with. It reminded me of a river that was overflowing its banks and flooding the surrounding land, which should have been used for farming or buildings. The brain needs to be able to input, process, assimilate the information and talk back to the rest of the mind and body. Broken connections and overloaded pathways were causing areas to be inaccessible and separated from one another. At the same time, his overloaded sensory system was needing boundaries, so he didn't feel everything from everything and everyone at the same time.

Father, I lift up the land of his mind to You. Life is being suppressed and held back in suspension. No mind can mature without having boundaries Father. My son needs those now. He needs to be freed from feeling every emotion, every noise or voice, feeling everything around him all the time. Father the world around him dictates what he feels and it overwhelms him so I say no more to it. I ask, Jesus, for your blood to cleanse his mind now and to rearrange everything, putting it all back in place. Father, I believe you have gifted him and that gift needs boundaries now. I pray Father, you will teach him how to live within the boundaries you have set out for him and intended him to have. I ask that you will free his body from being over run with sensations he can't control and that his mind will know a peace that passes all understanding. The water that is supposed to feed and grow the seeds of ideas, creativity, maturity and stability in the land of his life are being overrun and he cannot reap a harvest. Please, Father, set him free in Jesus' name now. You have gifted him, and you have blessed him with a strong mind, so I call those seeds to come to life, to rebuild his life and mind. Build up the banks of the river so it will not run over into every area of his life and ruin the growth. Set the seasons and the pathways for the river to flow in and may the land of his life be rich with blessings that he can handle. Father, I thank you for my son's strength, his creativity and imagination, and I bless the land of his life in your son's name Jesus Christ. Amen

Roads to be built with good foundations

I saw the roads like a network of neural pathways. When you build a road, it needs to have good foundations; otherwise, the road can crack, shift with weather and be unusable. So I prayed over the foundations of the roads, blessing them:

Father, I pray for the network of connections right now. I lift them up to you and I pray for them to be fortified and to be made strong. Father, you know the blueprints of man's mind. You built the mysteries of the brain, yourself. You were there when my child's pathways were laid out. You saw him forming inside in secret, and you know him already.

I ask that you would now strengthen the foundations of the roads of his neural pathways. I pray for strength, I pray for protection, I pray for health in Jesus' name over his mind. I pray for more connections, more roads to be built and that new pathways will be built, reaching out from one place to another so that there is no place that does not have a road to and from it. I trust you that you do everything with love and gentleness. Father, I plead the blood of Jesus over my child's mind now and ask for him to have the mind of Christ now, in Jesus' name. Amen.

Connecting brain areas to one another

Those roads represent communication lines, so every part of your brain needs to talk to each other. God never intended for there to be isolation or separation within your brain. Although there are different areas and different hemispheres, there is a divine order to his blueprints. We need to stay connected in the body of Christ just as the mind needs to be connected to all areas, too. So I prayed for the different areas of the brain to no longer be isolated, and the connections to be made.

Father, I pray connections over this brain. In Jesus' name, I pray against isolation and instead release the opposite to appear. I pray pathways and life-ways to connect from one side of the brain to others, from all sections to one another. Let no area of his brain be isolated or disconnected to others. I pray for blood vessels to connect and to flow with the light of your love. Jesus, you know what this brain needs, so I ask that you will release it all now over him. I pray for proper alignment in Jesus' name.
Where there are correct pathways that have not been used enough, I pray for them to come alive, be opened up like a highway that's been repaved and can be travelled on now.
It is as if they were one-lane roads that do not support the needs of his mind, but now there will be six-lane highways. I pray for life and life in the full to come to this brain in full abundance. I pray for more and more neurons to travel those pathways now, and I command his brain to come into alignment and enlightenment to God's plans now.

As each section of brain connects to one another, I speak strength and increase and blessing on each. Jesus, let your Spirit himself walk along the pathways and bless the neurons to increase in connections. I bless this brain in Jesus' name and release the power of the risen Christ over him. Amen.

Increased neuron activity

I speak to the neurons and all the matter inside Jordan's brain. I bless you, in Jesus' name, and plead the blood of Jesus over you. I say to you, increase, in Jesus' name. I say in Jesus' name, be free, free from being held back or not functioning properly. I tell you that there will not be a lack, there will not be low numbers, and you will not be sluggish but the strength and the numbers will increase right now, in Jesus' name. I remove sleep and sluggish behavior from them. I pray for blessings and increase now. To all the things that hold them back from firing and all the things that had decreased this activity, I say get out and stay out, in Jesus' name. I speak release over them. Be released to function as God intended. The brain that we are entitled to have because Jesus died on the cross is now superimposed over your head, in Jesus name.

I superimpose the blueprints of how God intended our brains to function now over my child's head. You will have healthy thoughts and healthy memories and your neurons will be healthy, in Jesus' name. Amen.

Eyes and hearing to be connected to brain

I felt like Jordan's ability to see and hear were somehow wired wrongly. They appeared to be working because he could hear us, yet he felt the sounds painfully throughout his body. He could see fine, but bright lights would overwhelm him often, causing him to close his eyes or scream in pain.

While on the other hand he found it hard to shut his eyelids to rest. I felt like something needed to be done with his hearing and sight. He heard everything from a dog whistle up to the T.V going on, yet other things went unnoticed and got lost in the translation. Sounds and light overran his nervous system and overwhelmed him every day and that was not normal or conducive to a good life. I focused my prayers on his eyes and ears next so that they would connect up to his brain in the right ways. He was having trouble sensing, processing and then responding.

In the name of Jesus, I ask God for you to come and touch his brain now. Lord, will you re-wire his connections between his eyes and ears to his brain? Please will you help them not be overwhelmed and overrun with sounds and lights to the point where they shut down. I pray, Father, for boundaries to be established now and to be obeyed in Jesus' name. Will you saturate his mind with your presence so that he can see and hear as you intended him to. Please help him, Jesus.

Let the world not overwhelm him, let his hearing and sight be connected in the right way to his brain so that the rest of his body can function properly with the information it's being fed. So I ask, Father, for the connections from ears and eyes to brain and from brain to the rest of his body to fall into normal parameters in Jesus' name. I bless his ears to become not only ears that will hear the world around him but also that he will hear your voice clearly, Father, and know you. Let his eyes see and interpret the world around him as he also is called to see miracles, signs and wonders and your face, Father God. I call the ears and eyes to attention and declare that the purpose for which they were created, is now in effect and that they should follow the design and blueprints of Jesus made for them. I pray and declare all this in Jesus name, Amen.

Mirror neurons

Even as a baby, my son neither mirrored what we were doing and largely never noticed us. In therapy, no matter how much we all tried, they could not get him to mirror anything they were doing.

The research on mirror neurons is quite interesting, well worth a read into it, but in any case, I decided to pray in what he needed because he was needing to activate them so he could learn from the world around him instead of ignoring it.

Father, I lift up his brain and especially his mirror neurons. Father, it seems as if they are asleep and not working properly, but you called us to speak of things as if they were and not as they are. So I pray for mirror neurons to increase in Jordan's brain, in Jesus' name. Where once there was a limited number, there will now be a larger amount. Where there were blockages keeping them from getting to parts of the brain that needed it, I release and remove the pathways to let them through.

In the name of Jesus, I say life to you all. Grow, grow, grow, grow, grow, in Jesus' name. Grow in number, grow in speed, grow in area traveled and coverage, grow in capabilities.

Where he once could not copy, he will observe and copy, in Jesus' name. The pathways will connect, his muscles and nerves will connect and get all the messages, his body will be as it was created to be, in Jesus' name. His eyes will see people, his mind will hunger to connect with people. Neurons, I bless you, in the name of Jesus, and I tell you to be healthy, in great number, in action and purpose, in movement and in connections. In Jesus' name, Amen.

Attention to flow in proper channels

After a few months of praying through the previous things, I had another vision. I saw the picture of a strong, fast moving river, flowing but it was breaking its banks and flooding the surrounding areas. When the river swelled and broke its banks, it had no boundaries to stop it flooding the land. As I was thinking about his attention needs and hyperactivity, it occurred to me that this river indeed was like the channels of his attention and that it needed prayer. I turned this vision into a prayer for his creativity, his concentration and his attention.

Having the ability to pay attention means having the ability to draw from a well of resources, to create life in the land of your mind and life. I used my words to pray for the river to be contained by boundaries and for this river to be channeled.

Father, thank you for the strength that Jordan has and that he has a great wellspring of ability to learn and observe. Father, I thank you for his creativity that you have given him, and I bless it, in Jesus' name. I pray for you to come and help heal the land of his mind so that he can pay attention, that his mind will have life to the full. I pray for you to give him the strength not to be pushed around where his attention leads him, but that channels will be opened in his mind that will bring life from one part to another.

I pray for you to give him strength to pay attention, use his attention and creativity through those channels. Come and saturate his mind, fill him with peace and shalom. Calm the pace of the imagination, creativity and attention inside of his mind now. Let the river that flows be free from fear and let it be allowed to flow in peace feeding the land of his life. Teach him Father, to channel the attention, to build up the banks and boundaries with love and peace so that life can grow and flow. Father, in your son's name I say peace be upon him in Jesus' name. Amen.

ADD/ ADHD

ADD/ADHD is the most common thing heard in doctors' offices with kids today, the most drugged and also the most misunderstood. I did not want to give my son drugs for a problem that God could solve with prayer. I really wanted to see what God said about this problem and see what he wanted to do about it. I knew that he was for the most part just being a boy, and naturally he had more energy, but not having the ability to rest at all during the day or night can be dangerous for anyone, especially those with growing minds and bodies. My son, who could not stop moving, did not have the ability to rest and stop. He was awake most of the night and cried all day.

Most children know how to listen to their own bodies to a certain extent, but for a child who doesn't feel connected to his own body and is not aware of his own signals for things like eating, sleeping, and going to the bathroom, it is a little different and his needs more help, or boundaries. He didn't know as most kids don't, what a boundary is. I believed one of the biggest influences that affected the way he was functioning was fear. The brain was never meant to function with fear in mind but with love instead. Your neurons, your pathways your entire body was wired with love in mind. The moment fear flows through your body it changes your hormonal/chemical makeup. For that reason I wanted God to have a Love encounter with Jordan. I wanted God to overrun his mind and pathways with the Father's love that there was no room for fear or anything else such as allergies that affected his attention levels. I felt like my prayers were to release a re-wiring of his mind. So while I took care of his diet as best I could (no sugars in his diet), I prayed against fear distorting and robbing him of peace and the ability to see things and not miss them.

Lord, I lift up his brain to you, now and I speak to his mind. I lift up this problem of hyperactivity and the deficit in applying attention. Lord, fear thinks it can steal, rob, destroy from my son his capabilities, maturity and relationships and has done for too long. It stops here. It has distorted his gifts and has removed his grounding in peace and love. Please give him the capacity to control himself and not to be agitated, but be freed by love and peace instead. Where he is lacking a boundary to control himself and slow himself down, I ask right now for you to give it to him and help him notice that boundary. I know that you don't want ADHD to be in his life and for it to control him with fear. Father give him a Love encounter with you. You fashioned our brains to flow with love and not fear, so I pray that you will demolish the affect that fear has had on his pathways, in Jesus' name. I pray that you will fill his mind with love and shalom. And that love and shalom will flow through the pathways of his mind now, love to flood his brain, love to flood his spirit, releasing him into freedom now. I release the shalom of Christ upon this brain. In Jesus' name, I speak to his brain and I release the kingdom of heaven upon him. Your kingdom come and your will be done, on earth as it is in heaven. In Jesus' name, Amen.

The mind of Christ

First Corinthians 2:16 reads that we have the mind of Christ. I thought I should not only claim that for myself but also for my son. I prayed this after I had prayed against ADHD/ADD because I wanted to superimpose the blueprints of Jesus' mind over my son's.

Precious Lord, I want my son to have the mind of Christ. I ask, God, for the brain that you created for us to have before the fall of man in the garden of Eden. Everything that was lost in the garden, Jesus got back for us when He died on the cross, so I come boldly before the throne and I want to ask for that mind. For the wholeness, the strength, the fullness and for everything that you designed for us to have, I ask now. Lord, I ask for it, in your name Jesus. And for you to give it all to my son. Give him a new mind, a new brain and a new way of thinking. I ask for a new way to deal with life, a new outlook of his world and a new strength because of the cross of Jesus Christ. You said, "Ask and you shall receive," so I have asked. I know you to be good and full of love, hope and healing, so please bless him with a new mind and way of thinking, In Jesus' name. Amen.

Spoken word curses

If we really grasped the power of our words, we would watch everything we said and probably wouldn't say as much as we do. I have never heard Jesus say to me, "Oops, I didn't mean that. Sorry that came out the wrong way." Who God is, is tied to what he says, and what he says is what he does. He stands behind his words constantly. He never says something then withdraws into hiding, taking his support with him. The Gospel of John describes Jesus as the Word become flesh. I believe that you should treat your words as all prophetic. You create what you want to live in by speaking it out so I had to really take a good long look at what I say, when I say it and what thought or lie is behind what I say. Your mouth has reproductive power!

The Word became flesh and lived among us. We gazed on his glory, the kind of glory that belongs to the Father's unique Son, who is full of grace and truth (John 1:14, NIV).

When God created the world, he used his voice and the power of those very vibrations created matter, planets, trees, land, biospheres and even the intricate intestines of an ant. He then made Adam in his own image and likeness. Our very vocal box is a copy from the original voice box of God himself. Our voice and words have power and can create things. What worlds are we creating for our children to live in?

Death and life are in the power of the tongue, and those who love it will eat its fruits (Proverbs 18:21).

We should watch how we label our children and we should watch what we say to them or around them. What doctors, friends, or teachers at school say about them can be damaging to them. The doctor can be temporally right in his/her diagnosis, but saying it in the present tense and the future tense in the same sentence can be a curse in itself. Diagnoses should only be said in the past tense, not in the present or future. I decided that I would try my best to be very careful only to speak life over Jordan and to break off any words that didn't bring him life.

Father, in the name of Jesus, I break off word curses spoken over my child. I release him from the words spoken over him that have been said to hold him down, that won't let him be free and are not promoting life. I break off words that speak of a future that is not in the mind of the Father. I break off words that people have carelessly spoken over him without the knowledge of the power of creation that comes from their lips. I break them all off of him, in Jesus' name. I remove them from his identity, I loose them from his memory, and I break them off his DNA, body and brain. I release him from alignment with those words and free him now in Jesus' name. I tell them to go, in Jesus' name. I say they are not you my son. They don't belong to my son, they are not part of his identity and they have to leave now, in Jesus' name. They were not you and will never be you, because Christ has set you free.

Lord, forgive me when I have labeled my son, and forgive us as parents when we have tried to put our children into boxes so we can feel more comfortable with who they are. Please forgive us and have mercy on us, Lord.

I call my child precious, whole, clever, wonderful and a gift from God. I call my child a privilege to care for and a privilege to have in my life. I call him a treasure and a child of God that will serve God all the days of his life as the prophet Samuel did. I say that you, child, will succeed in everything you do. You will learn at rates that will astonish us all, you will overcome all obstacles that try to come in your way and you will leap over adversity as if it was a pebble instead of a boulder. You will grow healthily in body and in mind, and you will laugh and bring freedom to people. You will hold fast to the peace that Jesus gives you and when things come against your character you will know who you are. I say to you, Jordan, know who you are and remember who you were made to be. You are a child of God. You are loved and wanted, you are precious and perfect, and you are going from glory to glory. I speak words of life and the kingdom over you and release heaven over you instead of words of lies and death. Amen.

Common sense

I prayed for him to have common sense a lot, as most parents would! There were basic things that he needed to observe and grasp through common sense for his own safety. I prayed for things like not running out into the road or into cars, and that if he didn't want his head to hurt, then he would have to stop hitting his head. If he was hungry, then he would have to concentrate and get the food in his mouth, instead of getting angry at me for it not reaching his stomach. While he ignored me, and others most of the time, sometimes he would walk off with complete strangers in stores without any fear. I would turn around, and he would be gone and would find him walking off talking to himself etc. Although he was still young at this stage and had a lot to learn, he still didn't have any sense of what was safe and unsafe. After a few of those instances, I stepped up my prayers for common sense and wisdom. He may have only been a kid, but wisdom poured out on youth is never wasted.

He must have been around 5 years old when something happened one day during home school. I felt as if God wanted to give him something, so I stopped what we were doing in schoolwork and asked him if he would pray with me. I told him that I felt God wanted to give him a present. Jordan agreed, saying, "Yes, Mommy." He closed his eyes and I prayed over him, first in words and then in tongues, and I asked Holy Ghost to come. I kept my eyes open as I prayed and I noticed that he had raised his hands in the air and started to play with something a little way above his body. I saw in the spirit something floating and coming into his hands. I asked him if he saw anything. He nodded, and said that he did. A few seconds later, he giggled and pushed his hands down into his stomach as if trying to feel something in there. He opened his eyes, and looked at me, smiling and laughing, as if he had been in a huge tickle fight with Jesus. I asked him what he saw. He said that he had seen a pink colored brain coming down from heaven that went into his stomach area. He laughed, because he physically felt it come down into his stomach. After he described it all to me, he pulled up his T-shirt and touched his belly to feel around for any change. He looked at me with a smile and said, "Okay, thanks Mommy." He jumped up and got back to his schoolwork. That was it! Simple.

Father, I lift up my child to you and I pray that wisdom and common sense will right now be activated within his mind. I call it down from heaven and ask that it will be rooted in his life, activated and growing now. I ask that his eyes will be opened. I call his brain and all his physiology, his neural pathways, his neurons, into alignment with heaven right now, in the name of Jesus. His mind will have the pathways it needs to get the common sense from the brain into his spirit and soul to the body and flowing properly. What he is lacking in, I call it down from heaven for him now. In the name of Jesus, I ask for everything he needs to have a healthy brain and a normal functioning mind. I plead the blood of Jesus over his mind now and ask for a complete cleansing of his mind, will and emotions. Amen.

Prayer for a relationship with God

More than all the healing, I saw that Jordan needed his own relationship with God. That is something I have no control over, but I do have an influence to show him who the Father is, how to interact with Holy Spirit and his presence, etc. Once he could handle church and being around worship music, he started to read his bible every day, but he still needed to see the loving Father behind the stories. It's the desire of every parent who already knows and loves God to have their children seek him, too. But God isn't an invasion army; he never will force any children to accept him in their lives. Often God patiently waits for them to make a decision to see him. Although Jordan had seen miracles and had experienced his presence, he still needed to be aware of Father God and his need for him before he could ask to have him in his life.

Father, I pray that you will never let my son out of your sight, that your eye will never wander from him and your presence will always be with him. Father, I place a hedge of protection around him drawing a boundary line in the land and say that he is yours, set apart for you. Father, I pray that in the right time he will seek you out and find you, that his heart will surrender to you and you will have a deep relationship with him. Forgive him for the things he has done and will do. May your lovingkindness always follow him around and may your love and favor be upon his life. I ask that when the time comes for him to confess he needs you, that his heart will be soft and not hard. God show him how to be your son, your friend and show him how to worship and love you. He needs you every moment of his life. There will never be a day when he doesn't, so I ask for you to have mercy on him. Please, Father, follow him, whisper in his ear, woo him, mold his life, teach him /your ways, love him like no one else ever can. Be his father and call him your child. Show him your heart for him and win him over. I dedicate my son to you in Jesus' name. As Samuel was yours from before he was born, so my son is yours, too. Thank you for the privilege of bringing him up. Forgive me for where I have let you down and not done things correctly. May your grace cover my parenting.
May my son's heart beat for you, Lord, In Jesus' name, Amen.

Chapter 14

Declarations

Honestly before this stage, I never really understood the whole declaration thing. I came from the thinking that the glass was always half empty. I had spent most of my life unknowingly declaring negative things over myself and my future as well as believing lies that were being fed to me. When I started declaring things over Jordan and our lives, it was like pulling teeth. It was completely unnatural to me to say positive things about myself, or our future. I felt like there was a spiritual war for my thought patterns going on, but that was because I was struggling with the orphan mindset. The things I was starting to declare over Jordan were simply the truth, but because I had listened too long to lies it wasn't a naturally easy thing for me to speak out. So as I learned to see God, myself and my son differently, declaring things became easier. Honestly it took me years to make the change in my mind and for me to think differently. I would often run back to God and ask him to please help me realign my vision so I could declare the his word and heart over my son instead of what my disappointments were saying.

Declarations should be made with pure, faith-filled words of truth. The spoken word is prophetic in nature, where they provide a platform for the things you are speaking out to land on. What you say about yourself and speak over your future will be life building a path in front of you to walk on. If you don't want it in your life then don't speak it out of your mouth.

After months of declaring stuff over my son, it was hard to continue because I would not see any change. So it was a battleground for faith. The bible's definition of faith is found in Romans 10 v 17:

"Therefore faith is from the hearing ear, and the hearing ear is from the word of God"(Aramaic version).

I would pace around my house declaring to the house, to my son and to the earth. I began to love the power of declaring. I loved to raise my voice shouting out the promises of the Lord over myself, my house and my family. I would wait till I was alone and start calling things out with great gusto! I am sure my neighbors heard me but I didn't care! Declaring is a form of prophecy, so I used my words to speak over things in my life and my son's. We are building up our children and not tearing down; we are to be a blessing to them and not curse. I wanted everything inside my son and in the heavenly realms around me to hear what was going to happen. I wanted the declarations to go through to every cell and molecule of Jordan's body. I wanted the enemy to shudder with fear at having their assignments cancelled. I wanted the earth to jump for joy because a child of God was taking dominion. I wanted my son's brain cells, his memory, his grey matter, and his muscles, nerves, neurons and everything within him to hear what I was now declaring over him. Even though there seemed to be no immediate fruit at hand, I was going to keep going until I saw the tree of healing manifest right there in my living room! My pastor, Bill Johnson says, "Nothing happens in the kingdom without first a declaration being made." I declared the plan of God to the world around me, in my family's life, my finances and my health and future.

Some Bible verses about your words and the power of your mouth:

Proverbs 18:21 (NLT)
The tongue can bring death or life; those who love to talk will reap the consequences.

Proverbs 16:24 (NLT)
Kind words are like honey--sweet to the soul and healthy for the body.

Ephesians 4:29 (NIV)
Do not let any unwholesome talk come out of your mouths, but only what is helpful for building others up according to their needs, that it may benefit those who listen.

Luke 6:45 (NIV)
The good man brings good things out of the good stored up in his heart, and the evil man brings evil things out of the evil stored up in his heart. For out of the overflow of his heart his mouth speaks.

Declarations of life

The Lord has not given us a spirit of fear, but of power, love, and of a sound mind. My child, I tell you that nothing shall put you under, nothing shall overpower you, nothing shall hold you back and no one shall tell you that you shall not be able to do things. Because I say that he that is in you is greater than he that is in the world and that you can do all things through Christ who strengthens you. I declare to your brain, have life and life in the full. You will rise up and be blessed. I declare that your brain is being healed, and God, who started this work in you will be faithful to complete it. I say to you that you can do all things through Christ who strengthens you. I say that you are wanted, you are accepted and important. You are wonderful and you are loved by me and by God. I say that nothing can separate you from the love of God. I say that your brain is normal and healthy and has everything it needs to live a life of serving God. You are amazing, child, and I say, rise up and call yourself blessed.

Declaring blessings

I speak a blessing over Jordan's speech and say in the name of the Lord Jesus Christ, you will increase and be blessed and function properly as you were supposed to. The speech centers of your mind will now have more activity; they will engage your memory and other areas that need to have articulated and appropriate speech.

I tell the blood vessels, in the name of Jesus, to increase to those areas and carry more oxygen and nutrients to where they are needed. I speak healing and blessings over your speech center, in the name of Jesus, and I say rise up and function as you were supposed to. I say the old ways are not good enough and are not to be visited; the old ways of talking are not to be used. I speak development over you, in Jesus' name. You were not made to not grow and be stagnant. You were made to grow and learn and become who you are meant to be. In the name of Jesus, the flow of creativity coming into the speech center, which used to engage itself to talk to yourself and inside your mind, is no longer the source. I say that desire to interact with people is now the motivation for talking. Wanting to interact and learn and listen will now stimulate the purpose for talking. I ask for a cleansing of the creativity that feeds the need to talk. And I ask that it will be made pure and connect with the right influence now. I release all these things, in Jesus' name. Amen.

Blessing the brain

I declare that you shall have life, my child. I declare that you will not merely survive but live a full life. You shall have life in abundance and to the full. You will have everything you are lacking in now. You shall overcome every lack and need, in Jesus' name and in the place of the ashes of mourning, I say you shall have joy.
*I declare that you are redeemed, in Jesus' name. I declare your brain is redeemed. Where there is lack, you now have fullness. Where you were floundering and trying to survive, you are now flourishing and working properly. I declare that you are **whole**.*
I speak the shalom of Christ over you and your brain. I declare that you will lack nothing in your brain and in your life. I declare that you are healed, in Jesus' name. I declare that you are an overcomer.
I declare that you shall have life and life to the full. I say to this mind, for all you have lost, you shall have a double portion; for all your pain you shall have double joy; for all your broken years, you shall have double the amount of years in life and opportunities.

For all your lagging behind, you shall have acceleration; for all the years you lost in speech, you will have an acceleration in speech and will speak like a wise older child. I say you will have speech beyond your years, growth beyond your years, fun for all the years of pain, friends where there were none, acceptance where there was rejection and wisdom beyond your years. I command life, life, life and more life to come to this brain. I declare it, in Jesus' name. Amen.

Chapter 15

Engage

I had been praying for nearly three or four years. I constantly prayed through each vision and declared over Jordan. I saw small changes in response to the things I had prayed through and from the changes in his diet, and daily and nightly routines, but I still felt like there was something missing. I was doing everything I could physically. I was praying the way God told me to, and I was fasting and declaring. I had changed our whole lives and home around, yet it felt like I had reached a brick wall and could not break through any further.

When I looked at my son, there still seemed to be a disconnection deep inside of him. When I looked in his eyes he seemed distant and withdrawn. There was an emptiness that I found it very hard to look into some days. I felt that he was in there somewhere, but I couldn't quite reach him. I could see his body growing, and I could see he was trying to interact with us when it suited him. I saw him trying to learn and speak in small ways, yet there was still a connection missing. It appeared that he didn't care or wasn't listening, but I knew that he was lacking the ability to sustain connection with the world.

People with autism have a blank stare, and somewhere deep inside is a whole human being trapped. It's not the usual far off look people get when they are daydreaming; this look is different. You can feel the difference. I was determined never to see that far off stare in my son's eyes as his normal way of looking. There is nothing about it that is okay or feels good. There is nothing about that disconnection that is peaceful; it plain hurts to see that look in a child's eye.

When I look at someone, I often get a feel for the person. I tried and tried to get him to look at me, to talk to me, to tell me something that I didn't have to coax out of him, but it never worked. I wanted to connect with him, but he wasn't wanting to connect with me.

Once again, after months and months of getting frustrated, I went to God and just let it all out on him. I had fasted, prayed, and researched and was doing everything God told me to do, but this brick wall that I had hit and was butting my head up against was tormenting me! I told him how hurt I was, I told him that what I was doing wasn't changing things the way I thought it should. I cried, I jumped up and down and got angry. I walked into my bedroom in tears and just screamed, "Where are you?" I collapsed on the floor in a mess and refused to move until I heard from him. Once again, he answered me with another vision. This picture was like something out of a science fiction show. At first, I didn't know what I was seeing. I saw three identical figures of my son. I could see them, all lined up, behind one another. They were swaying backwards and sideways, as if on different frequencies. I instantly knew that one was his body, one was his soul, and the other was his spirit. When I looked more closely, I saw they were different. The color and density of them was different. They seemed to be moving in different phases. I didn't really know what it all meant.

I stopped and pondered the vision for a while. I didn't want to rush the revelation of it all, so I asked God to show me what he meant. As human beings, we are three-part beings, comprised of body, soul, and spirit. We all have these different parts, but when I looked at my son, his parts seemed like they were all out of phase with each other. It looked like every now and again, they all came into sync for a split second or two. Then, as soon as they phased together and had come into alignment, they went out again and were off on their different frequencies, moving in different directions. People who have dealt with autism know what it's like to see that disconnection and the blank stare. God was showing me what was going on inside of Jordan and with that understanding, I had direction on how I was to pray for him.

I had a new prayer point to ponder over. His body, mind and spirit were not connecting to each other; they were not engaged, and he needed to be in alignment. A person can be fully alive and present; yet all three need to be connected and not separated to have a fully engaged life. Autism seems to split a person from being a triune being into a fragmented individual that struggles to interact or connect with life. The spirit and soul seem damaged or stunted in growth, and the body keeps growing.

My goal after I saw that vision was obvious now, to pray for the spirit and the mind of my son back into alignment. My new prayers were for Jordan to become integrated and engage, live, and connect with us. Whatever happened to make him split, God could fix. Whatever he needed to integrate himself, God could fix that, too. There were a lot of "what ifs," but I knew there is a bigger God, who can fix those "what ifs."

<u>Reintegrate</u>

Father, I speak shalom over my son's spirit, soul, and body. Lord, I ask for him to be anchored by your Holy Spirit and fused and connected together. Lord, I pray the conflict will end, and I pray for the peace to come and flow through all of him. Father, please put him together again.
I speak life to his spirit that it may take charge of his life and that he will learn to engage it and that it will be strong and healthy. Make him whole, and help him engage his life. As for his body, I pray that it will have peace to house in harmony the two as you intended from the beginning. I pray, Father, that you will heal the damage that made them split. I pray against it happening ever again and I ask, Father, for the healing frequency to be released over his mind now.

I pray against the splitter that has come to separate and destroy and has done damage to his life. I place a hedge of protection around him and remove any hooks in his life that the enemy would use to pull on, to pull him out of alignment again. Instead of discord, I release the spirit of wholeness and completeness, the spirit of shalom over him, in Jesus' Name. I ask for the Holy Spirit to come and dwell in him now and to fill his spirit up with life. I ask for your blood to anchor his spirit, soul and body together now. For life to come, in Jesus' name. Amen.

Chapter 16

Encounters with heaven

Heaven isn't just somewhere you will have everything that you have ever wanted, like a lifetime supply of chocolate that doesn't sit on your hips. It's not about the place where you never have to clean your house ever again (although I am looking forward to that) or where your pet hamster from childhood is waiting for you once you get past the pearly gates. Heaven isn't about all the hardships, the bills, the "interesting" family Christmas' disappearing, and where everything becomes about YOU and what makes YOU perfectly happy, forever. A healthy desire for heaven is about being with the one who is at the center of it all. To me heaven is about being a family again, being with Father God, having fun and loving everyone who's there perfectly. An appropriate desire for heaven is not based in a morbid, cowardly escapism mindset, where you want to run from life on earth to a place where things are easy forever. If your hunger, your view and your need for heaven is not centered around Jesus, the Father and Holy Spirit, then you have the wrong picture of what it is about.

As a child, I was naturally drawn to heaven and Jesus and everything about God. One of the first times I remember seeing Jesus and coming into contact with the supernatural was when I was a child around 3 or 4 years old. I was alone in my room playing with my Barbie dolls on the floor. I had them sitting on my dollhouse chairs, lined up in rows while Travel Barbie led a church service from the front. She was leading the worship and praying for the other toys to be healed. In the seats were Darth Vader, Darth Maul and Luke Skywalker, who were temporarily borrowed from my brother (much to his annoyance). A few of My Little Ponies also looked on with eagerness from the sidelines, but as their legs didn't bend I couldn't have them join the others in the seats! I do believe they were all healed of something that day as it was a totally amazing church service!

While I was sitting there in mid-play time, I remember turning to my right towards the window that overlooked the back of the house, and I saw Jesus walk through the wall. He was as bright as the sun, so bright that in fact I found it hard to look at him and so natural as if he did that kind of thing every day. He walked towards me and then knelt down to sit beside me on the carpet. I remember not being fazed at all by what had just happened. His presence didn't make me scared to the point where I ran out screaming. Nothing about him walking through the wall and into my playtime worried me. I just carried on doing my excellent voiceover acting of Barbie praying for people and Darth Vader being healed and coming to know Jesus. It seemed a pretty perfect time to turn up actually if you think about it! He asked what I was doing as he sat down beside me and crossed his legs to watch the scene in the toy house. I told him that they were having church time! I pointed out that Barbie was healing people as she prayed for them and was leading them in worship.

Looking back now at that scene, the thing that astounded me was that no one had taught me what a healing service was. I could barely tie my shoes and talk! I didn't remember going to church as a child, I had not been exposed to revival culture then and no one had ever taught me what Jesus looked like. If you think about it, what child at 3 ish plays healing services? Everything in me *knew* that he was Jesus. I don't remember how long we sat there playing together or what we talked about, but I remember him. I was struck by how time stood still and how peaceful and natural this whole situation was. He stooped down to my level and came and played with a little girl and her "My Little Ponies" one morning while she sat alone and imagined what it would be like to have heaven on earth.

That was the first time I saw Jesus with my physical eyes. For as long as I live, I will never forget that first meeting with him. I remember the look of the smile on his face, how gentle he was and how he just came to me to play with me. From before and after that moment in my childhood, every cell of my being knew him. He made complete sense to the young child that I was then. No one had to teach me how to talk to him or teach me about heaven or the Bible for me to know who he was.

Everything in me that day relaxed and said I was home when I was with him. That set the tone for our relationship. That was a point star by which I was guided for the rest of my walk and life with Jesus. He was free to walk in whenever he wanted and rock my world. There were times he did turn up in my room or life and I physically saw him; there were times when I had dreams and visions, encounters with Holy Spirit that remain signposts in my life. I had prepared my whole life to spend it ministering to him and for him. I had spent my teenage years training to be on ministry teams, praying for people, working for the church. Later on when I was a little bit older I went into YWAM and travelled to many countries, but none of that really prepared me for the challenge that arose in my relationship with him after my son was born.

I tried to draw on the wealth of ministry training, prophetic training, missions training, but nothing quite fitted my mothering a special child. I had no scope for what I was living through. None of my training prepared me for this and I was floundering! When God asked me whether I would stay with him no matter what, I could see the look in his eyes again—those same eyes I saw that first day as a child in my room playing with the toys. I had lost purpose behind the training and serving, I had the wrong set of eyes for the job ahead. I needed to change and see my situation from heavens point of view amid the praying and therapy and diet control.

I was beginning to feel alive, hungry again for more of him. Hunger always costs something. And I grew extremely hungry for another encounter with Jesus and heaven, like I used to have before my son was born. I started to ask for meetings with God face-to-face, I wanted to hear his voice, have more revelations and insights, I asked for gifts and an increased prophetic gifting, but the thing I grew hungry for was a trip to heaven.

I was searching around online for people's stories of their heavenly encounters when I found a video of Jesse Duplantis talking of a trip he had taken to heaven. It was called, "Close Encounters of the God Kind." The title immediately sparked my interest! I watched the video over and over again and then bought the book to make sure I didn't miss anything. In it Jesse talks about his encounter with God and a time when he was transported to heaven for this life-changing trip. The things he described made me cry because that month I had been asking to see those very same things.

It made my faith and hunger rise. He had been asking to see God face-to-face, and one night God had actually turned up in his bedroom to meet with him. With curtains flying in the air, the sound of a heavenly wind and a presence that felt like it was going to rip the flesh off his body, he was confronted with having to turn around to see God's face. As Jesse had asked for this meeting and to see him face to face, Jesse found that he could not do it. Jesse could not turn around. As a result the presence of God left his room and went back to normal leaving Jesse alone. Months later, while on a ministry trip, Jesse was having lunch with the pastors before he was due to speak that evening. He felt a sudden urgent need to go back to his room to be alone with God. He excused himself from lunch and made his way back to his hotel room to pray and be with God.

Within seconds of kneeling in prayer on the floor of the hotel room, he found himself being transported to heaven. He walked around, talked to some very well-known people, and saw the Lord. He had a tour, saw houses and ate fruit from the trees that lined the streets and river banks. He was literally gone for hours. When the experience was over, he found himself still kneeling in the same position in his hotel room only a few hours had passed. It is an incredible story.

That night, I went to bed with the expectation that God was going to do something for me like He had done for Jesse. I had asked for years to see him face-to-face, and this story only made me dangerously hungrier. As I drifted off to sleep, I had the thought, "Maybe tonight, maybe." At 3 a.m. I woke up to the feeling of someone poking my right shoulder. Tap, tap, tap. I wondered if I had done too much wrestling with my son earlier and now my shoulder muscles were twitching! As I was half asleep, I didn't know if I was just dreaming, but again it happened. I was lying in bed alone, sleeping on my stomach, with the covers pulled up to my shoulders when I felt it again. Tap, tap, tap. I slowed my breathing down and tried to listen to see if I heard anyone was standing beside me, but I couldn't tell. I didn't want to turn around because I wasn't sure I was ready to see what exactly was poking my shoulder. While I could no longer hear the wind blowing outside my window, it was replaced instead with the sound of my heart loudly thumping in my chest. I seemed to have mislaid my courage!

Courage just got up and left plain old"me" to address what was poking me. Again, poke, poke, poke. I was now fully awake and alert, and yet purposely pretending to be sleeping (putting my years of acting training to good use). I became acutely aware that I was not alone in my room. There was a presence in my room. I had asked God to do what he had done for Jesse and even laughed at the story because he freaked out and wouldn't turn around. I said arrogantly to myself, "If that was me, I would have just turned around." But now, it was my turn. I had asked for God to visit me in the same way he had Jesse and take me on a trip to heaven. I felt like he had actually turned up and was now prodding me to wake me up.

I felt the poke one last time, only this one was a little harder and faster. I knew that it wasn't my husband because I could hear him downstairs. I didn't want to turn around and face whatever was poking me at that time of the night. So, I said quietly, "No, I can't turn around. I am too scared. Please go away." In an instant, whatever was by my side of the bed was gone and the room's atmosphere was back to normal. I plunged myself under the covers and thought, "I asked to see the Lord and when he came, I told him to go away! I did what Jesse did, too. I am so sorry, Lord. It's just dark, and I am too scared at three a.m.!" I felt so bad. I was fearful and had freaked out. I didn't know what to do because if I asked for another visitation then maybe he might turn up at 3 a.m. again and I might react in the same way. I didn't want to waste this hunger or his precious presence with my uncertainty, but I wasn't sure what to ask or how to continue to pray for this.

I have learned in my walk with God to be specific when asking for something from him. I usually think carefully before I ask for anything because I am not in control of the way it is delivered to me. I don't try to outsmart God with the way I ask for things because I will never be able to do that. But I have learned when he asks me what I want and if I am not specific, then I should get ready to strap my seatbelt on and prepare myself for a fun ride. I had asked God for a visitation, and he had shown up. I wasn't so specific on the details of my first request, so the second time, I worded it better. Instead of asking God for another visitation from him like he had visited Jesse, at 3 a.m, I said, "Can I come up there?" Amen.

That prayer started something, because all of a sudden, things started to change between God and me. Things started to happen, revelations about God's word and mysteries were being shown to me. On one night at about 3 a.m., I was sleeping alone in my bed. A winter storm was raging outside the window, and it was very cold in the house. I was fast asleep when I awoke to the sound of loud knocking. *Bang! Bang! Bang!* For reasons I can't explain, my body immediately reacted, and inexplicably I found my body sitting up straight in bed. I rubbed my eyes and was trying to understand why I was awake and secondly why I was sitting up when the last thing I remembered was happily sleeping under the covers. Why was I doing that? Then I remembered the sound: like a big thumping sound or a knock on a huge thick heavenly door. I knew that that sound wasn't my front door being pounded on by someone in the night. But I had to check just to make sure, so I crept out of bed and over to the window that overlooked the front door and I saw no one. I crept back into bed then I heard it again. *Bang. Bang. Bang.* This time I got afraid and looked down the long, dark hallway towards the rest of the house, which was pitch dark, I might add. I didn't know if I should move and walk down the dark hallway, get on my knees and pray, or wait or go back to sleep. I knew that God was summoning me, but honestly I was too scared to move again. Ultimately, I summoned my courage up, and said loudly, "Yes, Lord. I am here."

A long silence followed. I waited for what felt like nearly five minutes with no response. So I got up out of bed and waited as I prayed and paced my room; then I felt like God was saying, "Come up here."

So I replied, "Come up there? Where? How? When? Is there something you want me to do, Lord?" The only problem was that I didn't know where "there" was or how to get up there! I heard nothing back, but decided to wait under the covers instead as I was starting to get very cold pacing in my PJ's. I almost expected a portal to appear in my room or an angel to appear ready to escort me, but nothing changed in my room. I waited and waited, staring down the long, dark hallway that led to my son's room. Nothing happened. The banging stopped.

In the morning, I woke up wondering whether it was a dream or not. But deep in my spirit, I knew I had heard that sound. It reminded me of a court announcer from hundreds of years ago, the man with the long heavy stick, who would bang it and shout the announcements out to people coming into the presence of the king. That banging sound stayed with me clearly, as though the sound was lodged in my spirit. I knew I had been summoned before the King, but I didn't know what he wanted me to do or how to go see him as he had asked. My thoughts turned to Queen Esther from biblical times and all that she had to do to prepare to appear before the king. Maybe God was calling me to prepare for something before I saw him? Maybe I needed some time to get ready for what was coming? I started to read up on all the preparations that the priests in the Old Testament went through before being ordained to serve and found out that they started service on their thirtieth birthday! *Hmmm,* I thought to myself, *there is something on that,* and I felt God smiling as I found a clue as to what he meant. Somehow they were tied together. It was indeed not far away from my 30th birthday! Sneaky, sneaky God! He was indeed building up to something, and I had a feeling that it was going to be a fun few months of preparations ahead of me.

Months passed after I prayed that "More Lord!" and had heard the "come up there" when God had started to radically invade my life. He had intensely stepped up his visitations; countless times God woke me up at 3 to 4 a.m. to tell me things, show me passages in the Bible and explain revelations to me. One day out of the blue the Lord asked me what I wanted for my 30th birthday. Although it was over six months away, I thought it was strange to be asked so far ahead of time. Something I have always done since I was a child was to write a long letter to the Lord for each birthday. I reflect on and thank him for the previous year of work in my life and look forward to the new season.

When God asked me what I wanted that year, I started to think about it and thought that as it was my 30th, I should have 30 gifts!! That sounded perfect to me. On the top of the birthday wish list was a trip to heaven, second was a holiday away with God alone, and the third was a gemstone from heaven. Among the other things on that long birthday list was something that I had wanted to do since I was a child.

It was to train in worship or go to a worship school. I went to some pretty amazing churches growing up; the worship departments were always packed with talented and gifted people, and I had been involved in small ways. But I had not fully stepped into my dream of being involved in worship. I had laid most of those dreams aside when my son came along because he needed so much help and attention. I had always asked God growing up if I could go or get more involved or train in worship but God had always said, "No, not yet." I had now been waiting for 17 years. After all those years of doors closing and God saying "no, not yet," I had lost the excitement of wanting to go until in the middle of struggling to plump the list out, I remembered my dream. So I added it to my list of wishes for my birthday. Why not? I thought, *What's the worst he can say.. No!!*

I had been getting the sermon of the week from Bethel Church for a while when one day I decided to look around on the ibethel.org website. I was on the main page when I saw the advertisement for the school of worship that started on my 30th birthday. My heart just about flipped! I so wanted to do something like that but always in the back of my mind was, *How can I go anywhere when I am needed at home and taking care of Jordan and his needs?* I was totally torn between dreaming with God and the practical needs of my family. I screamed with joy and asked God if I could apply, but I didn't hear anything back from him. I waited and asked for a sign or confirmation, a Bible verse or for him to tell my husband I could go. I talked to my husband and he was excited for me but I hadn't the money to go. God had said no for over 17 years, so I thought it would really be a miracle if I got into this one. As I didn't hear a yes or a no, I figured that I would test the door and apply anyway. There were some obstacles to getting in, I needed references and application fee, etc. But I got it all organized and got a reply! I had been accepted!

I could not believe it, I had waited so long to do this, but I was a little nervous about leaving my son with a nanny and my husband while I went off on a break with Jesus. I had a lot of preparation to do if I was going to leave my son alone with my husband for a month. I had organized his homeschool work for the month, his activities and games. I had lunches and dinners planned, cooked and ready in the freezer waiting to be re-heated.

I had organized his therapy sessions and had a nanny to help take care of him part-time. All the money I needed for the school came in and I had the plane tickets booked. I was ready to go. While I was getting ready to go and preparing myself for the holiday with God, I heard the Lord start to speak again about "coming up there" but I still had no idea what He was talking about or how to get up there. One day during one of my quiet times, the Lord whispered to me that for my 30th I was going to have 30 days off with him up the mountain. Also up until that day I had everything turn up for my trip in 3's. Someone gave me $300 for my trip, I had sold an instrument for $300, the Sky Miles I used up for the plane tickets were 30,000 miles, etc. For a girl who loves numbers that made me very happy!

I had arrived at Bethel Church! The first church service I went to there had me in tears! I had not been alone or been able to go to church for years so it was so amazing to sit down for an entire service but this one was even more special, I had turned up on Father's Day! I was ready to start my classes and to learn all I could from the sessions and people there. One of the first sessions at Bethel's worship school was taught by Judy Franklin, in which she led us on encounter trips to heaven. And there was my trip to heaven from my wish list! As Judy taught and shared her story, she described her visions and how things began in her journey. You can read her journey in her book, *Experiencing the Heavenly Realm* (Destiny Image Publishing). She had us all pray and soak for a while as we focused on Jesus' face. The next thing I knew, a faint vision entered my mind's eye.

First, I heard the sound of wind blowing in the trees gently. Then I saw a picture of a tree branch swaying back and forwards as it was touched by the wind. After that, I saw a tall gray brick wall standing at about 10 feet high. A tall, majestic weeping willow tree was standing in the far corner to my left, gently being brushed by the wind. Under it was a Victorian white cast iron table and a chair with a glass of lemonade on it. I didn't see too many other details, but I got the feeling that the rest of the garden was unfinished, waiting for something. There was no way I could make that all up even if I tried. I had not come up with that vision from my own imagination; I was not thinking about any of those things, so I knew that God was in the driver's seat.

I'd had many visions before, but it was as though this one was different and almost interactive. I could walk around in the vision and look at things, touch, and experience it all. It only lasted a few moments and then I was gone. I found myself sitting up from where I was lying on the carpet as if I had just taken a cool catnap.

I expected visiting heaven to be more physical and tangible, as if I left my body or something. (That is the kind that you don't really want to do too early if you know what I mean!) This, on the other hand, was more in a sense, a vision or a dream. It integrated both my vision, my senses and my creativity into imagination submerged in Holy Spirit. There was no doubt in my mind what I had seen. I had just had my first trip to heaven!

The school days were filled with great sessions and teachers, one of whom was Dan McCollam. Dan has an amazing teaching on the physics of sound and worship; it completely reset my thinking of God in science and in worship. He got to a part where he was explaining how they can be healed with sound waves, how music affects the body, etc. I started thinking to myself, "What if autism can be healed with a sound? What if God has a sound that can sort that all out?" A fire of questions and hunger set off inside my mind. What if God could do this? I was deep in thought and questioning God about what I had just heard, so I went out to get a drink of water and take a walk to think my questions through. As I left the sanctuary, I decided to sing in tongues as I walked out to the lobby. I was saying in my heart, "God I want a frequency that heals autism. I want to see it gone from my son's life." When I returned to the room, I heard Dan say, "What if there is a frequency that will heal autism?" I just about fell over! That was like pouring fuel on my request for God's fire. I wanted it; I wanted the answer. I wanted the frequency, the sound, the song or whatever God's answer was for this. Whatever it was, God had the answer, the song, the sound and the secret, and I was going to ask Him for it!

Sometimes important questions need to be asked at a special time and not in a quick passing moment. I kept that secret deep in my heart and told no one about it. I wanted to seriously seek God's face on this one.

The answer, if he decided to give it to me, would shake my world to the core and possibly other's too. So I kept that question in my heart for a time when God and I would be alone, and I carried on with the rest of the training in the school. My time at the worship school and Bethel Church was just about over, and I had to head home. I had learned so much from not only the church but also the school. The teaching was incredible and changed my life. I felt like I had an infusion of new DNA into my being, and I would never be the same again.

Chapter 17

Home + heaven = heaven

When I got home, I had to transition quickly back into housework, unpacking, homeschooling, errands, and therapy sessions. I had missed my son and my home. I looked at him, hoping there would be a difference in his face or behavior, maybe a change or a growth, but he was no different than before. When I looked at him this time, instead of feeling the pressure of prayer and doing all the home school and therapy work, I looked at it with a different mind. The challenge had changed for me, with that thought of "Maybe there is a frequency or a sound that can heal autism" running through my head, my faith of expecting God to turn up and do a miracle had grown. I picked up where I left off in my prayers and continued to bless and pray for him.

A few days after I got home, I found that I was really missing the Bethel prayer chapel and the great number of hours I spent on the floor there soaking. My mommy duties didn't make room for soaking times that lasted for four hours! So I grabbed them when I could. When I came home, I created a prayer room in our spare room in the house. I filled it with 24/7 worship music. I would soak and pray either at night after everyone had gone to bed or in between lessons during home school. I would spend a few minutes here and there just praising or singing and resting in God's presence when I could. Jordan would see me lying on the floor singing, praying or reading my Bible and would often just come sit beside me. He just wanted to be near me because there was a lot of peace that saturated the room when we praised and prayed. My son liked my prayer room and liked sitting in there because it was so peaceful, and God's presence was so thick in there. Sometimes I would actually home school him in the prayer room, surrounded by the soaking music, which helped him concentrate and relax more.

A few days had passed since I got home. I was going about my usual duties around the house when I felt an unusually strong desire to go into my prayer room and to be with Father God. I felt like God was waiting for me in there, so as I walked into the prayer room and said, "Yes Lord?" I felt God smile back, as if he had been waiting in there for me to turn up! His presence was so heavy. I felt like he wanted me to just be with him and that he was waiting for the question I was holding onto in my heart. "What if there is a frequency that will heal autism?" I thought to myself, *now's the time to ask him* so I knelt down and said, "OK Father, I am ready to ask you that question now. What's the frequency my son needs to be healed?"

Almost audibly I heard, "2.5 delta."

At first, I wasn't sure if I was hearing that right, or if my imagination had made something up. I asked him to repeat what he had said, but that number would not leave my mind. It was somewhat familiar to me as I had heard it somewhere, but still I thought, *What am I supposed to do with that number?* Was 2.5 delta a frequency that Jordan's brain needed and couldn't make on its own? Or was it the exact frequency that kids need to be healed of autism or just what Jordan needed? I just didn't know. But that is what I heard. I ran downstairs to grab my neurology books and started reading about delta waves. The whole day had turned into one great fun research assignment in the prayer room. I felt as if Holy Spirit was there, helping me by opening up my mind to understand all I was reading and reviewing.

Most of the research I had found was, unfortunately, based on new age relaxation and sleep aids. I didn't want anything new age or based in the world to go into my son's brain, so I put down the books and decided to go to God instead. I said to him, "God, I don't know what this frequency is exactly or how I am to make it for him, but I know he needs something from you. I don't want a frequency from down here based on the earth and from new age medicine. I want it from you, directly from your voice box and heart. No sound is good enough down here for him, only yours is. God, help me. Please show me what I am to do now. Amen."

A few days after that, I walked into my prayer room to do some painting and praying when my son walked in to see what I was doing. I heard the Lord say, "Bring him up here (heaven)." I said, "Can I do that with a child? How do I do that?" He replied, "The same way you came. Bring him up here." Then I saw a set of keys come down, and they were handed to me in the spirit. They were huge, old, solid gold keys. I was in the middle of the vision of seeing the keys being handed over to me when Jordan came into the room. I asked him if he wanted to go on a trip to heaven to see Father God. He nodded yes. It neither scared him, nor bothered him at all. I laid him down beside me and got him to close his eyes. When he was settled, I had him repeat a prayer after me. He kept his eyes closed, and as we finished the prayer, I asked Holy Spirit to come. I placed my hand over his head and prayed in tongues for a few seconds. Then we waited. With his eyes closed, he put his arms up in the air above him as if to touch something floating above him and then he giggled to himself. I gave him a few moments before I asked him again what he was seeing. When he did open his eyes, he told me that he saw a shimmering sparkly cloud coming towards him. It went all around him, and it tickled him. I told him that was God's presence. He said he wanted to paint what he saw, so I gave him some paints and a little canvas, and he painted it.

A few minutes later, I asked him if he would like to go again. He said he would. I laid him down again, and this time, he went immediately. A few seconds later, he opened his eyes and looked at me. He told me that some angels came and flew with him through the stars. I asked him if he wanted to paint it, and he said that he did. He painted a few stars in space, with a few angels' wings. He looked up at me after he was done, then ran off to play with his trains! The supernatural was so normal for him. Jordan simply opened up his spirit and mind to God, and the Lord met him. And that was it, the first trips to heaven. It was as real and as simple to him as anything could be.

Trips

The trip to heaven that changed our lives happened that same day at night before bedtime. He'd had his usual routine and was climbing into bed when I heard God say, "Bring him up here. I want to sing over him."

I was so excited and asked my son if he wanted to go on another trip up to heaven before bed. He said, "Yes, please." I told him to lie down quietly and close his eyes. I asked Holy Spirit to come as I prayed over him in tongues for a minute or two. I asked God to take me where Jordan went and to show me what he saw so that I could confirm what was going on. We prayed and confessed our sins and lay there soaking in God's presence for a while and then I told him that if he saw Jesus, to take his hand and walk with him. He said he saw Jesus walking towards him through a cloud and that he took him by the hand. As the three of us walked through a glittering cloud, I could see a pair of golden doors up ahead. I asked Jordan if he saw some doors and he said yes. I asked him what they looked like, and he started to describe them to me in detail. I told him to walk on through the set of doors, one of which was cracked open and light was pouring through the opening.

The magnificently shaped arch doors appeared to be 15 feet tall and made of solid gold. I followed right behind him, and then we stood in what looked like a huge room that was light, alive, and shimmering. It was a long, big room, filled with gold that was clear yet solid, crystal-like, yet not see through. (It's hard to explain.) I asked him if he saw something on one end of the room. He told me yes and that he saw a big chair. I could see what looked like a stage area with a few steps leading up to the top of the platform. I asked him to describe it. But before the words left my mouth, he said, "Ohhhh, Mommy! It's a rocking chair!" I asked him if he could see who was sitting on it and he said, "It's Father God." I told him that if he wanted and felt comfortable, he could go and sit on his lap for a while. He said that he wanted to and as he lay in the bed, I saw his little legs running sideways under the covers as he ran towards the Father, who was waiting with open arms. I followed him and went around the back of the chair to see the Father holding Jordan on His lap. I heard the Father say, "I love you, Jordan. I love you, Jordan," as He lovingly rocked him back and forwards in his arms.

I said, "Jordan, what is Father God doing now?" Jordan told me exactly what I had just seen, that Father God was holding him in his arms and rocking him, telling him that he was loved. I could hear the gentle voice of Father God talking to Jordan as he rocked him in his arms. I could hear the Father's voice saying things to Jordan as he snuggled up against the chest of the Father. For the first time in his life, I could see my son calm down and rest in his body and mind.

It was as if all the tension in his muscles left; his body was finally experiencing rest and he lay there calmly just enjoying it. Normally, I would have to help him calm down, hold his body still for him or massage him, but this time I was doing nothing but watching. A few minutes passed while he rested in the Father's arms, and I just waited as I sat beside his bed on the floor. Suddenly, I heard something in the spirit, a very low and faint sound. While I was still watching Father God holding Jordan, the sound came from around us, like a hum or a tune. It reminded me of the part in the Magician's Nephew by C. S. Lewis, where Aslan the lion was creating in Narnia with the low hums and melodies. That low hum also reminded me of the Bible verse in Genesis that talks about Holy Spirit hovering over the face of the waters at the beginning of time. I wasn't sure I was hearing anything at all because it was so low, yet I could see something happening around us. I asked Jordan what was happening and if he was hearing something. Jordan said that he heard the Father humming over him.

After another few minutes, I saw Jordan's hands rise in the air above the bed covers. He was playing with something just in front of him. His hands appeared to be going up and down in a wave pattern, but I couldn't see what it was or why he was doing it. I asked him what he saw and he said that he could see a wave coming towards him that looked like an x-ray. He continued to giggle and play with this wave that was coming towards him. As it got closer and closer, he smiled widely yet still his eyes were closed. Jordan said that this green wave was coming from the mouth of the Father and went into him. At that point, Jordan grew very peaceful and quiet and within a few seconds, he fell deeply asleep and started to snore. This had never happened before; it usually took hours to get him to sleep, hours of him talking to himself, flapping his arms or shaking and distracting himself in the dark or jumping around his room for hours before he collapsed somewhere. But this time, he fell asleep on the Father's lap, in the heavenly encounter, as he was being held and sung over. I sat beside him for a few minutes, singing in tongues and just letting God do what he wanted to.

I felt such peace in his bedroom that I didn't want to leave. Thirty minutes passed, I had been sitting beside him the whole time praying and listening to Father God sing before I finally kissed him goodnight and walked out.

I shut the door to his room and was in awe of what God had just done. It was amazing that my son could see the spiritual realm so clearly, without fear or doubt. I went to bed wondering about that experience and was eager to see more of what God would do in my son's life.

The next morning, for the first time ever, he woke up at a normal hour, got out of bed and walked into my bedroom and said, "Good morning, Mommy." !!!! You have to remember that he would wake up at 5 – 6 am and pace somewhere in the house or his room for hours talking to himself, flapping his arms, eyes fixed at a point in his imagination and with hardly any clothes on to keep warm. That was all I was used to until that morning. I just about fell out of bed in shock! For the first time ever that morning, he came to me and said, "Good morning." He jumped on my bed and hugged me and we snuggled for a while. I was secretly crying as I held him and was so happy. Later he sat down at breakfast, looked me in the eyes as he ate his breakfast and talked to me about the dreams he'd had. It was amazing. After years of prayer, this "thing" that you could see on him or behind his eyes was now gone.

It marked the beginning of a season of heavenly trips on which God took him on walks around towns and down streets, showing him more sights and sounds. On one of his nightly trips, Jesus took him for a walk down a street and we saw people smiling and waving at us. They said hello to us and called us by name. We saw houses, streets, parks and huge buildings. Every time I went with Jordan and stayed a few feet behind Jesus and him as they visited places together. I asked to do it that way so I could see everything as well as be a witness to it and remind Jordan of it later. Each time, he woke up and told me what he saw. Sometimes, he drew what he saw. Sometimes, I would draw it for him so he could always remember his visits with Jesus. After that point, the Lord said to me that it would only be a season of him coming up to visit. I never wanted it to end, but I had to obey the Lord's wishes. After a season of about 6 months of daily visits when he would walk through a glittering cloud, see Father God and sit on his lap, walk with Jesus around, it was over. But his life never went back to the way it was before. He was forever changed.

Eventually, he was discharged from his outpatient special needs therapy because he had met all the therapy goals, which he speedily conquered. To me, he was completely different from the years before. That distant look in his eye, that disconnection that separated him from life had gone. People would also look at him then and comment on how that look—the "whatever" it was—had gone. For years he was shut up and locked away inside of himself, peeking out from time to time; now he was observing life happening all around him. Although he had to catch up on everything he was missing out on, most of the changes were slow and small to the untrained eye. That heavenly encounter was the start of the big changes in his life.

Chapter 18

Signposts

It was easy to focus on just the autism at the time because it truly was a monster to deal with. It had taken over all my focus in my prayers, but that left two other major health challenges too: allergies and hyperactivity. When God asked me what I wanted and I had replied that I wanted to see this autism thing gone, I had the other 2 ugly problems at the back of my mind, too, but I could not go after and take out all three at once. I mean, they are the most diagnosed and medicated problems in our children today, and I was just one little mother in her prayer closet! I felt that picking on three giants at once was a little too much and probably not so sensible, so I decided to go after one at a time. I picked autism first. As the autism was going and he was recovering and playing catch up for all the things that he had missed out on. I started to target the allergies next.

The hyperactivity was actually tied into his allergic reactions. When one raised its ugly head, the other came out to play as well, wreaking havoc for weeks on end. Now bearing in mind, one of his worst allergic reactions was nuts and egg products of any kind. Just the smell of it and boom, hives and hyperactivity for a week! But that was the way we had lived; we had accommodated them in our lives and had gotten used to their ugly faces turning up every day. Even in the midst of Jordan's heavenly trips, and the constant years of praying for him he would still have breakouts of hives and skin problems, but I reminded myself that I was indeed going after one thing at a time.

Around this time my marriage of nearly 10 years fell apart and I could not fix it all myself, no matter how hard I tried. Jordan and I had moved and were trying to rebuild some kind of a life for ourselves. I was left to raise my son alone in a new place alone. When we did move,

I noticed that his allergic reactions were lessoning. Where once we could not go to parks, places that had nuts or eat anything with nuts in, now we could go to a park and play. We went out a lot, parks and hikes, we were at the beach and played with other kids and went to children's church — all things he could never do before. While he had mild reactions all the time, his recovery time from the mild allergies were shrinking too. We were enjoying more of a life for the first time.

One day I had a birthday cake that was sitting on my kitchen table. It was meant to be taken to a friends birthday party later on that day but proved to be a huge distraction for Jordan. Until now, because he could not ever eat those kinds of things, he had gotten used to not asking for any. But for some reason, Jordan, who had been eyeing it up for hours, for the first time in his life asked for a piece. I looked baffled at him and thought to myself, *Where have you been for the last 7 years son?*

But I replied, "No sweetheart, that's Franky's birthday cake, and you know it has eggs in it and you are allergic still." For some reason he didn't give up this time; he really wanted a slice. So he continued to ask me for some for the next four hours straight every 10 – 30 seconds! And I repeatedly answered, "Sorry, no sweetheart." At about the 5th hour, I had had enough and got tired of the constant questioning. I closed my eyes and said, "God I am out of patience. He keeps bugging me, and I keep repeating myself. He is not listening to me. Help me! My parenting skills are running on empty. This is your problem. You deal with it. You are his father first."

God said, "Give him a taste,"

To which I replied, "WHAT??!!!"

God said again, "Give him a taste."

I did think to myself, *Where have you been, God, for the past five years? Don't you know what we have been through and all his problems? I have been praying, and you haven't done anything. What are you talking about "give him a slice of cake"?*

But with a slight bit of attitude, I replied to God, "Fine, whatever reaction he has, you have to take care of it, this is all your problem and all on your shoulders, YOU are his father." (I sound like a nag!)

He had accidently eaten things with eggs in before and the reactions were milder then a nut allergy for him, but although we had seen a huge change in his allergic reactions, I was extremely hesitant and had never done anything like this before. I would never recommend for people to do this, but I strongly felt the Lord say to me to just give him a small taste. So I went into the kitchen and grabbed his allergy medicine in case what I was hearing was completely wrong.

I said, "Son, come here. It's OK. You can try a bit."

You should have seen the smile on his face. I bet he was thinking, *Oh dude, all that nagging Mom finally worked!* I cut him a tiny piece (mostly frosting!) and handed him the fork. He shoveled the cake into his mouth, and said, "Thank you, Mom" and walked off skipping. Usually even the cooked eggs in a baked good would still make him break out immediately in an allergic reaction around his mouth and torso, so I ran after him, checking his skin and face to watch for the usual reaction to unfold. We waited patiently, clock ticking in the background. I stared at his face, Jordan looked at his body checking for hives, and you know what we saw? *Nothing!*

I searched his face and body a couple of minutes later and again nothing. There was no reaction. Jordan also knows what to look for so he was watching to see if he was itching anywhere. And he didn't.

"Dude," I screamed with joy, "have a bigger slice!!!"

He was only too happy to oblige me. I gave him another taste this time with more cake and less frosting – NO REACTION. Next I gave him a bigger slice and still no reaction.

We screamed and jumped around the house thanking God and doing victory dances in the living room. This thing had ruled our lives — and dictated so much of what he was to do, where he was to go, what he was to eat — had been beaten and sent packing with one simple answer from God.

But that got me thinking, *I am going to test this*. So I ran to the fridge, grabbed some eggs and immediately started to make some separated scrambled eggs. I made him some egg whites and nothing; then I gave him just the yolks and still no reaction.

To this I strapped on my apron and started to bake as if white flour and sugar were not the enemy! I baked him brownies. He ate some and had no reaction. I made him scrambled eggs for dinner with bacon. Again, no reaction. In the morning, I made him crêpes for breakfast. Still, no reaction, whatsoever. Cookies, cakes, and everything else I could think of produced no reaction.

You have to understand that this is something that we had lived with for seven years, every day, even multiple times dealing with it during the day. We had been used to having his allergy medicine in tow at all times, carrying his Epi-Pen with us (which thank God, I have never had to use because we watched and took care of him well) and having a clean up routine ready to go if anything happened while we were out. This was simply a total miracle!

Why do we make healing so hard to understand sometimes! I think we make it more difficult than it is supposed to be. That day I followed God's lead and I let God take care of it, which he did. There was no laying on of hands, no pleading with or begging God (although I did all those things). I just said, "You take care of it," and he did. It was simple enough for a child to understand.

Since then, he has been lucky enough to attend school and sit next to a child who had a pbj sandwich for lunch. He can be in the room where nuts are and he has had no reaction.   We have been able to go to parks and play. We have been able to play in the dirt, rocks and soil and have no reactions, either, whereas before the dirt, the pollen, the dust, walking among the trees—all would have him scratching, screaming in itches and red blotches all over his body, not to mention the tantrum caused by his clothes wet or dirty. He has been able to eat things that he hasn't been able to eat before with no reactions, and the world is opening up to us slowly. He is still struggling with some minor animal and food allergies, but like the ADHD, I fully intend to see it leave and go back where it came from, leaving my whole son alone.

Chapter 19

The beginning of the end

From the very beginning of our journey till now, it has been more than five years. It all started with God asking me the big question. Five years of prayer, therapy, declarations and every day working with Jordan. It's been an amazing journey into God's heart. I saw a lot more than I put in the story here; there were twists and turns all along the way, there were set backs and heartbreaks, and even the enemy attacking me every single day calling me a liar and that Jordan would not be healed. Not a day went by when something didn't happen to try to pull me down or break me, but I would not change any of it because it brought me closer to God in the end. In God's mercy, he didn't leave Jordan or me in the state that he found us in, but he lovingly came after us both, healed us and made us who we are today.

There were two important things that I learned through this whole experience: 1) I learned who I was in Christ and 2) I learned how to pray from that place.

My prayer life changed because I finally understood who I was as a child of God. And secondly because as my pastor Bill Johnson says, "persistence in prayer doesn't change God; it shapes us for the answer," I can see that that is why I needed to change so much and be healed, too. It started with it being about Jordan's healing, but in the process it became about transforming my heart to know my Father more deeply.

My heart's desire is to see children and people who have struggled with autism and other disorders on the spectrum, heal and engage in life. If I were to only offer mine and my son's testimony to you, then I know for sure that you would be missing out on the other cases we have heard of. There are simply many more stories out there of people who have had the same amount of breakthrough, many not even in the same way as ours happened. No two healings ever occur in the exact same way.

Our church is one of the few places that I have ever been to that whenever it's either offering time or a testimony is shared, we all start jumping for joy or shout and yell. We rush for the buckets or grab for the offering basket when it's time to give or when someone gets up to share a testimony, we are all cheering them on and clapping at the purely wonderful and good God we serve. It's one of the many reasons I love my church so much; there is so much joy in what we do. We simply love testimonies! The bible says the "The testimony of Jesus is the spirit of prophecy" (revelation 19:10). So when a testimony is shared, you can jump on the back of it and take it for your life too. The breakthrough that someone else had, testifies of the power of the cross and who Jesus is and what he has done.

A good friend of mine has worked at Bethel Church as the testimony writer for years. Her job is primarily to collect the testimonies here at our church, either from inside our walls or from our church members who have been traveling or from churches we are in contact with around the world.
For this reason, I wanted her to share with you some of the other testimonies that she has collected of people being healed of autism and other disorders.

I shall let her tell you in her own words:

> I've been serving at Bethel Church as a testimony writer for almost six years. A few years ago, I received requests from people in three countries asking for testimonies about autism. At the time, I did not have any, but I took their names down and promised to get in touch with them if ever I did. Within a year, I had begun to receive autism testimonies.

The first one I heard about was reported by Barbara Kort, the mother of a child with Down Syndrome and autism. Her daughter was at a healing conference at Toronto Airport Christian Fellowship and heard a word of knowledge for the healing of a child with Down Syndrome and autism. She received a gift of faith and seized that word for her brother. She phoned her mom to tell her that her brother was healed and to lay hands on him and pray. The next morning, he awoke full of the joy of the Lord and began changing. Two years later, specialists determined that he was no longer eligible for services for the autistic.

I rejoiced and sent that first autism testimony to the people on my list who had inquired. Shortly after that, I received a testimony about another child in another state who was being progressively healed of autism. Then I met Lizzie and took her testimony. I was so impressed with this young mother and tenacious prayer warrior. We became great friends. And I see the healing all over Jordan. He always greets me warmly when I visit and gives me a hug. His life is a testament to the power of God.

Since that time, I've heard prophetic words about the body of Christ gaining victory over autism, and I've received an increase in testimonies from all over the place. One of the most striking testimonies I've heard of from a friend whose grandmother knows the family, took place, I believe, in Oregon. A mother had taught her autistic child to repeat all day long, "I'm healed. I'm healed." He was about six or seven years old. One day on his school bus, his mind simply cleared. When he got off the bus, he greeted his mother with the words, "Hi Mom. I'm hungry." He had never spoken like that to her; she was shocked. Her son, indeed, was healed.

It's remarkable that God heals in so many different ways. We know that healing exists because of the work of Jesus on the cross. Beyond that, there is no formula. Some are healed in worship, some, in declaration, some, after receiving prayer. Here are a few more recent testimonies I've received that illustrate the uniqueness of each person's experience of healing:

In Australia, a young man of 19 diagnosed years ago with Asperger's had been introduced to revival at the age of 16. Some time in the last year, he heard the Lord say, "Come, soak with Me." While he was soaking, the Lord said, "You don't need this anymore" and took that away. He was completely different after that, and they have undiagnosed him, pronouncing him free of Asperger's. His therapist said, "You are like a man released from prison." He is now an artist, musician and relentless revivalist.

A mother was reading *When Heaven Invades Earth* to her son, who has Tourette Syndrome, and he was healed.

In Fort Worth, Texas, a 17-year-old, who had been diagnosed with Asperger's as a child, and her family had left the church. The family came back to that church for a meeting with a visiting speaker, and the pastor hugged her, and she uncharacteristically allowed him to. She, also, was undiagnosed.

A severely autistic child, about seven years old, in Nelson, New Zealand, received prayer. From that day, the child's "meltdowns" started slowing down. His healing took place mainly over six months. Now the boy is completely restored and healed with doctors' reports to verify it. He has been mainstreamed back in school and has been experiencing no difficulties. The doctor discharged him from treatment. His teacher aide at school helps him get caught up, but doesn't need to do much. He is happy.

One of our church members has been leading a weekly prayer meeting for new brains for those who need them for whatever reason for a few years now.

About a year ago, God started showing the Bethel Healing Rooms leaders to expect healings of autism. He has shown some of them about the connection between worship and healing. He is saying that through that realm of touching a really deep place in worship, we will see autism and mental conditions healed more and more. We rejoice every time a seemingly insurmountable "mountain" bows its knees to the power of Jesus. Because of Him, there is hope for all. And of late our senior leader, Pastor Bill Johnson, has been seeing much healing to do with issues involving the brain. Let's all savor these testimonies and expect God to *do it again*!

**

I want our story to inspire you to go after God with all of your heart and to be a signpost pointing to heaven. There are many stories out there of healings from depression, to dyslexia, autism, to ADHD and ADD, and it just goes to show that nothing is too difficult for the Lord to heal. Areas that once we saw few healings in are going to become more and more common. We all need healing in different areas of our lives. No one is more of a mess than another person; We are all equal in his eyes and there's just a greater opportunity for a testimony of his work. In God lies the answers you need. In God lies your healing. In God lies your true home. I know that when you take a step towards him in surrender and hunger, he runs a mile to come closer to you. He loves you more than anything else in this whole universe. Nothing is more important to him than you.

So if you are willing, pray that God will invade your life and heart, and you will never be the same again. Make your own journey with God.

Go dig your own well with God, and make your own signpost to heaven!

Book recommendations

Johnson, Beni. *The Happy Intercessor*. Shippensburg, PA: Destiny Image Pubishers, 2009.

Johnson, Bill. *When Heaven Invades Earth: A Practical Guide to a Life of Miracles*. Shippensburg, PA: Destiny Image, 2005.

Johnson, Bill. *Face to Face with God*. Lake Mary, FL: Charisma House, 2007

Johnson, Bill. *The Supernatural Power of a Transformed Mind: Access to a Life of Miracles*. Shippensburg, PA: Destiny Image, 2005.

Johnson, Bill, and James W. Goll. *Dreaming with God: Co-laboring with God for Culturla Transformation*. Shippensburg, PA: Destiny Image, 2006.

Johnson, Bill. *Strengthen Yourself in the Lord: How to Release the Hidden Power of God in Your Life*. Shippensburg, PA: Destiny Image, 2007.

Vallotton, Kris, and Bill Johnson. *The Supernatural Ways of Royalty*. Shippensburg, PA: Destiny Image Pub., 2006.

Leaf, Caroline. *Who Switched off My Brain?: Controlling Toxic Thoughts and Emotions*. [S.l.]: Inprov, 2009.

Franklin, Judy, and Beni Johnson. *Experiencing the Heavenly Realm: Keys to Accessing Supernatural Experiences*. Shippensburg, PA: Destiny Image, 2011.

Duplantis, Jesse. *Heaven: Close Encounters of the God Kind*. Tulsa, OK: Harrison House, 1996.

Liardon, Roberts. *We Saw heaven*. Shippensburg, PA: Destiny Image, 2000.

Friends websites

Bethel Church: **www.ibethel.org**

Bethel TV: www.ibethel.tv

Bill Johnson Ministries: **www.BJM.org**

Beni Johnson: **www.Benij.org**

Kris Vallotton: **www.kvministries.org**

Moral Revolution: **www.moralrevolution.org**

1609065R00091

Printed in Germany
by Amazon Distribution
GmbH, Leipzig